Gabriel Benedict is not a theologian, scholar, or scribe. He is just a man on a journey who was blessed with an insight into suffering. His life is worth noting because his suffering can touch you, his story is your story on some level. Or perhaps you may gain some insight with someone that you may know. He believes that it is our common suffering that unites us. Gabriel battles mental illness, trauma, various social issues, and addiction. These are common elements, that in one way or another affect you or someone you know. He believes that it is in our journey that we may find a simple solution of love, acceptance, and forgiveness to be the time-tested solution for us all.

With all my love to my mother, my children, and all of the people that have helped support me in any way, through some darkness.

Gabriel Benedict

ALL I KNOW TO BE TRUE

AUSTIN MACAULEY PUBLISHERS™
LONDON • CAMBRIDGE • NEW YORK • SHARJAH

Ordering Information
Quantity sales: Special discounts are available on quantity purchases by corporations, associations, and others. For details, contact the publisher at the address below.

Publisher's Cataloging-in-Publication data
Benedict, Gabriel
All I Know to Be True

ISBN 9781645756835 (Paperback)
ISBN 9781645756842 (Hardback)
ISBN 9781645756859 (ePub e-book)

Library of Congress Control Number: 2021900462

www.austinmacauley.com/us

First Published (2021)
Austin Macauley Publishers LLC
40 Wall Street, 33rd Floor, Suite 3302
New York, NY 10005
USA

mail-usa@austinmacauley.com
+1 (646) 5125767

I have always been man of faith, even if I hadn't been the most faithful servant. That means that I realize my imperfect nature and total human condition, that being said, it is through faith alone that I haven't ended up dead. What little pride I have left is total self-preservation. Not in the sense of our current state of affairs in politics or religion, yes, I am about to speak of those two things we are told not to discuss. At this stage of my life I walk for the Lord, and the Lord only! Does that mean I live a saintly life? (I wish) I am, after all, only human. To my benefit, I have always loved truth, and I have always reveled in it. When a song strikes me and another person, or myself and another person enjoying a good book, quiet conversation or even a movie, that feeling of unity or sharing an emotion on the same level is so important to me. I have done many things (right or wrong), just to duplicate these instances or recreate the bonding I share with people or individuals. The reason I preface all of this before I delve into my journey. Is that no matter what absurd circumstance I brought upon myself, it was my faith that carried me through it. At the core of most of my actions was love, and the desire to be loved. It was my faith that yielded a hope, that has now become an expectant desire to survive any given situation.

Our nation is facing one of the most difficult times in our history. And as I write this, I'm moving with grace. That is not to say that I'm not scared. But it is through my faith that I can receive this grace of managing the times and which actions to take. I don't hesitate in times of need, and it has served me very well. When to move, when to retreat from a situation, or when to be bold. To me, that means being obedient to God's laws. And trying to do your best for others. In the simplest terms, I'm not God. I keep doctrine and theology very, very simplistic. I have to, because I'm prone to over analyze until I paralyze to the point of inaction. That to me, is just as deadly as resentment or self-pity. I don't have time for either of those in my life. As for my journey, faith has required a lot of action. It isn't as abstract as most would suggest, and for me it isn't just a random collection of prayers and disciplines, as I had once thought as a younger man. That being said, I did have to simplify and 'just do it' (sorry Nike; does this suffice as a footnote? I don't want to get sued, but it's all good; I don't have any money). Tangent aside, I remember my acts of faith as a child, and I'm remembering the things that I had faith in as a child such as: Mom's love, never going to bed hungry, the sun rising in the morning, and for sure, church on Sunday. Mom always took us. Without fail or excuse for not going (a discipline that I'm just now understanding as a 41-year-old man; I don't miss these days).

One of my earliest memories is running into the church aisles and getting pinched by Mom to shush or settle down at mass. I'm Catholic, received all my sacraments, and for the most part was a great catholic until the age of five. My sadness didn't start then, but my seditious behavior toward authority did. It wasn't in my mind random. As I was justified as I was getting hit on the hand with a ruler by a nun in Catholic school. I totally forgot to mention that I was being very disruptive in class. Kind of like running in the aisle at church and getting pinched. Please keep in mind that I have been battling this ego from birth. My rebellious nature has sometimes gotten me in trouble, and actually, my nefarious trait has served me well at times, in all actuality, more out of self-preservation than righteous cause. The righteous cause would be defined as being selfless and unassuming, or perhaps more ambitious. But in this instance, after many years of self-examination/therapy/ meetings, I realize what that meant; I had none of that. I see with clarity what that blessed mother was just trying to teach me, that I'm not God. Sounds simple, right? But what did I know at five? Other than in my own nature, I wanted to do what I wanted. Most would have listened and straightened out, but I chose the harder path. The path with most resistance in rebelliousness, and a dangerous individualism that almost led me to death on more than one occasion. It was this first choice that would alter my life forever, the first of many decisions on where my free will that was given to me by God, was self-serving, and instantly gratifying. The satisfaction of immediately filling a desire soon became my method of operation for most of my life. I went home and told my mom of this 'cruelty' and the next day, I was removed from that school in Omaha, NE. My mother always says that I was always preaching to other children at that age. That I was always filled with the Spirit. I agree to that point as well, but I also realize that my human condition, poor choices and misuses of my free will also became obvious at a very early age. My biggest disillusion throughout my life is that the mind is more important than my spirit. I have suffered from the most damning intellectual pride and fool's notion that knowledge is all power. I spent a majority of my life trying to illustrate that point of pride in reverse.

I have mentioned free will with much emphasis so far, I feel I should mention that I'm not a scholar, not a theologian; just an ordinary man on a journey, so keep reading if that fact is acceptable to you. As I am, writing this for me, I'm also writing with the prayer to reach just one soul. That is where I am these days. Just a steady rhythmic beat to help a brother or sister out of hopelessness, despair or depression. This world is so deceived and full of lies. That is a fact that we ALL can agree on; whether you agree with my faith or not. I can only share my view on how I rose out of the ashes of a war for our minds and souls. This world is wanting nothing more than to imprison our minds and take advantage of all of our human weaknesses by seeking nothing but a profit. Charity is nothing more than a tax write-off. Love is crucified and murdered, God on earth, Jesus. Our souls are made trite and inconsequential, or that war is the answer and peace unattainable. This is our common bond, whether you're Christian or not. This is why we fight together against one common enemy; the war inside our self, the struggle at its most basic level.

It can be called good vs. evil, or more like they taught us in school as far as literal concepts, man vs man, man vs nature, etc. All my life, I have had to fight. For some reasons yet known to me, I was one of those miracle babies. My mother tells me that for the last two months of my birth she had to be on bedrest. The last two months! Wow! A mind can sit and wonder as to what could possibly have occurred. As to my knowledge at this point, no one has been clear with me. And quite frankly, it no longer matters. As far as my childhood is concerned, I could've been born to a family of apes, swung from a vine and named Tarzan. In other words, I'm still trying to piece together my childhood. I use humor and sarcasm to deflect some things that are very painful to discuss. I don't care if it isn't the healthiest way to cope, but I've tried Prozac, and in fact, lots more than that.

I guess that my earliest attempts at self-control and self-medication began at the age of 12. That was the earliest time I can remember back in my childhood. I wonder why it is that I can only remember bits and pieces of my childhood. I used to think that was the status quo for most people. As I have come to learn it isn't. There are a lot of things that I thought were the 'norm.' For instance, I believed it was normal for a constant struggle to be heard, I thought it was normal to bottle up emotions, I thought fear was a constant companion to satisfaction, or that anger was scary. I also thought it was normal for Dad to only tell me he loves me when he was drunk. I guess I had some fundamental belief that in order to express myself, I had to be chemically altered. Kind of like The Weeknd singing, 'When I'm fucked up, that's the real me!'

That summer 2015 anthem really stuck with me. It almost gave me a justification for me to get messed up, then express my emotions, because that for some reason made them more authentic. When I had my first drink at the age of 12, I did it because that is what I saw my elders do. Self-medication and chemicals were the only way to gain control or some sort of release of my emotions. My family gatherings, from birthdays to Christmas always consisted of the men getting drunk and then usually breaking down to some form of immaturity to express some emotion that had been burning within them the entire night, or maybe even lifetime. After that repeated and crude indoctrination to this lifestyle and way of coping, it is no wonder that I turned to chemicals at such an early age.

I often think of the interior battles that I wage daily within myself. One of them is with depression and PTSD. I'm not a man who suffers more than anyone else, of that I'm sure. I also can say truthfully that I may suffer more in the future, who knows? I'm not afraid of suffering. In fact, I tend to thrive under pressure or duress. It seems like that is when I'm strongest. My weakest moments come afterward. My father has just recently passed. I don't feel much of anything about this loss. I have known for some time that he was ill. He had esophageal cancer. He fought for several weeks in the ICU in Austin, Texas. It has only been four days since I have found out. My faith has been challenged in a lot of ways this past week. March 1 2017, that is the day I found out about my father passing away. I have committed my entire life to do everything in the opposite of the actions of my dad. On the occasion of my being informed of his death, is the day I also quit smoking. I had been smoking cigarettes since I was 12 years old. I have experienced many forms of suffering in my life for sure! But throughout all of these sufferings, I have maintained a great deal of faith in God. As my father used to say, he always believed I was 'lucky.' I always begged to differ, that I was blessed. He and I were always at odds with each other. That is putting it very mildly. We never agreed on much. We were very different men. Although, we share the same name, that is pretty much where our similarities begin and end.

My dad was raised 1 of 14 children in San Antonio, Texas. He was poor, and the military was his ticket out of poverty, as it is for many of poor men and women. The areas of San Antonio that my parents were raised are to this day very poor. Anytime I'm in San Antonio, I visit the home where my mother was born. She was one of ten. So both of my parents knew poverty. They knew what it was like to suffer, and they both dealt with alcoholic parents. So it is no wonder to me why my mother stayed in this abusive relationship. It was probably the healthiest that she had ever known. Could you imagine living in a home the size of a 1,200 square foot apartment, with ten other children? So, when I look at this home now which is vastly different, I know that the life that my dad provided was probably better than any my mom had ever known. At least that is what I tell myself, to not blame my mother for staying married to such an incorrigible man.

Again, after the age of five is when I began my quest to rebel. I knew at the very core of my being that there was a God, even though since my birth, I came out of the womb a fighter. For some reasons not known to me, my mother was on bedrest for the last two months of her pregnancy with me. My mother was told that I was not going to make it, so my grandmother put my mother on bedrest and took care of her. It is no secret that I speak my mind and what I feel. There was a period of time where that wasn't possible at all.

I would say that around the age of 8, that things drastically changed. I lost my sense of self, it would seem. As I reflect on my childhood, it is extremely hazy. In fact, as I reflect on the good moments of early childhood, I find them few and far between. I have memories of school, but vague ones at best. For instance, when I would sit in class and daydream. Or images of wetting myself in front of class as an elementary student, because I was too afraid to ask for permission to go. Or memories of getting a cut on my hand and just letting it bleed all day during class, hiding it in my jacket pocket as for no one to find out, for the fear of asking anyone for help was too much to bare. Another vague memory is wearing an Adidas T-shirt and being made fun of. I haven't worn Adidas since. The powerful image I remember is that acronym, 'All day I dream about sex.' There is a pertinent reason to mention this because I went home crying. Children can be so mean without even knowing how cruel they can be. I went from being a positive outgoing child, to being afraid to ask to go to the restroom and wetting myself in front of the class. By this time around 1983, our family had been stationed to Fort Worth, Texas. There is a huge gap in my childhood because the next thing I remember, I'm heading to Germany. I was 12 years old!

What a vastly differently youth it had become. So, this age is so important because I rapidly learned how to kiss, lost my virginity and took my first use of chemicals (cigarettes and alcohol). From those days on, life was in 'high' gear. So began my acceleration of the fast life, and my love for it. This duality of vain existence conflicting with my very Catholic upbringing, encumbered with my abuse of free will. During that haze, I made my sacraments up to reconciliation. As things as far as my memory is concerned, become more in focus. I had apparently become a server for our church, I was in the boy scouts, participated in ballet folk dancing; it was also apparent that I was gifted, or rather had a decent amount of intelligence. For whatever that is worth, I know now that my dad didn't consider himself the smartest man or have a very high opinion of himself. I had also been playing little league baseball. Another memory that I remember around this time, is the fact that I could sing. My music director in school had recommended that I join choir, and that he would personally take time and give me lessons. To this day, my mom lets me know how I promptly declined. Then she would usually add it to my number of rejections of what a normal life she tried to give to me. See…at this point, I rejected the boy scouts, being a server, the Mexican folk dancing, the talented and gifted program at school, and the offer to sing and the instruction that came with it. The latter I remember that someone told me it was gay, so I quit. To my mother, I was just rebelling from all the 'good' things in life. To me, I was chalked full of fear. Ah, fear, that big little word that cripples the soul!

How my life was so full of fear! How fear dictated all that I would or wouldn't do at this point. I looked at home videos of myself at this time, and I looked distracted or disinterested in everything we did. From family trips all over Europe, or my birthday parties. For me, fear ruled my life. It ruled all I did (or didn't). All my mother, family, or extended family could see was that I never finished anything. Up to that point I just knew, I had this big hole in my heart that nothing was the norm and nothing could fill it. To top it off, I was afraid of everything. I'm also afflicted with prepubescent insecurity, shyness and a very mild manner. I was such a pushover just seeking validation, love and attention, as everything in my life from that point on was failure and insecurity. The old adage, 'If you don't stand for something, you fall for everything' is really resonating in my mind right now.

Up to this point, all I knew was fear, but why?

So, welcome to life as I knew it at 12. My rebellious nature surely kicked in. Again, I must reiterate that I have been a fighter since birth! All I knew of love was that of which was shown in my household. The bickering, the emotional pain, the alcoholism, the sobbing, the pleading for forgiveness and the instability. My extended family was no better, how is a child to thrive in this type of environment? I was in my late 30s when I learned that that wasn't normal. For decades, my perception was that this was what life was all about. Less than 72 hours since I have learned of my father's death, and here I am repeating the pattern I have so desperately run from. As fearful as I was in public and of the outside world, at home I was a different story. I had begun to stand up to my father, and what I perceived to be his lack of love and his disrespect of my mother and myself. At 12, I began to resent the fact that I was left to clean up and fill the void at home of the lack of love in our household. As far as I'm concerned, that is where I had my biggest misperception which was that of love. I was that awkward, nerdy kid that always seemed to try to latch on to 'love' anyway I could find it. Like that damn song, 'Looking for Love,' by God knows what puny country artist, my journey took off to find it. My faith dictated to me that I knew it was out there, and that there had to be something more than was in my home. I knew that my father was wrong in most of what he did and said. I knew that he was a liar, a cruel and inordinately mean. There are stories that I could bore you with of drunken ordeals and unabated pleas from my father for us to just love him. It was really quite traumatic for us all. At this point, my sister was four years old. I love her no matter what, but I cannot speak much for her, as she must've also been so affected by all of this going on around her as well. My sister and I aren't close, as we were so far apart in age, and to her credit, I know she must deal with things in her own manner. I totally respect anyone's journey in this life.

All I had known to be true at this point was conflict, strife, drunkenness and fear. So what is an impressionable boy to do? As we were leaving Germany, we stayed at a friend of my father's home as we were preparing to leave back to America. I was first introduced to pornography, but not by anyone, but rather of my own curiosity, boredom and lack of direction. I was alone while my parents went out with their friends. I was alone at my father's friend's home. I was looking through a pile of VHS tapes and I stumbled upon a porn scene. Now, this is pivotal in my sexuality because for some time I had already been sexually active. I naturally imitated the scene and was jerking off like the men on the film. I came within, what seemed like a minute. What was sick about my behavior is that it became a self-soothing cure for loneliness and boredom. It would become my solution for loneliness and full-blown coping mechanism, so thus began my journey seeking love through self-gratification and sex. It left the door open to years of shame and guilt that led me to blame my faith, and at such an early age it became a destructive coping mechanism. The instant effect of orgasm and relief of stress, or 'love,' as shown on the VHS. It is so foreign to me now, because of what I know love and sex to be. It was as if this sick way of self-love became all I knew at that point. Little did I know, that that way of coping was not right or natural. I mean not even animals in the wild do that, much less the 'evolved' human. If we are so great, why do we resort to such disruptive behavior?

Sex became my drug and favorite addiction. Not just masturbation, but sex as a whole became my motive and identity. Throw in the hormones of a growing teen, and I was off the charts horny, Catholic, and totally guilty and ashamed of myself. For my nonbelievers, have you ever seen an ape pleasure itself? I might have missed that episode of Mutual of Omaha or National Geographic. Maybe the late Steve Irwin missed that in his expeditions. I mean really, how can I resort to sex being the bane of my existence? I am a man, who by this time of my life, has done my fair share of self-pleasure and has done most manner of depravity. So, I believe that it is a fair question to ask. And if honestly answered, there are just somethings that our friends in the animal planet just don't do or 'rationalize.' The truth is, that our minds and bodies are what sets us apart. I agree with the science and biology of why our species is special, but isn't that what we all suffer from? Some manner of terminal uniqueness? This manner of needing validation, and making it the priority of our existence? I watched some absurd movie with Bruce Willis the other day. Something where he was blowing stuff up and yelling, 'Yippee kay yay!' Or something like that. The premise of this work of fiction was that some ultra-bad dude could shut down the whole country with a computer, and that the end of the world was at stake. It really struck me that we are so isolated and glued to this binary code of one's and zeroes. It dawned on me that people might actually believe this kind of fear mongering; that because we don't get our cell signal on time or that we don't have an automobile, that all of western civilization would collapse. I propose this: Would that be a bad thing? Wouldn't we be forced to draw our validation from something else?

I mention all of this in conjunction with my budding early sexual appetite, because at this point in my life, computers were changing all of our lives. The advent of cell phones came at a crucial point in my life. I had more freedom and far less grace with the combination of internet porn, hooking up, and now getting chemicals faster than your local pizza shop. I was also hanging out with the older crowd. To this point, I'm a very impressionable teen learning all modes of uses of chemicals, sex and false validations. Kind of like Facebook, but actually leaving my house. By this time I was 16 years old, and I had my first job as a waiter at a gyro restaurant. It is truly amazing, the kind of freedom that comes with a job where you always have money on a daily basis and a budding appetite for drugs. The sex just came with that lifestyle. As anyone who grows up into adulthood, it becomes more apparent that these are just vices, and for a more fulfilling life to be experienced, there is so much more than that.

There are moments that are hard to write about. This is one of them.

I have paused for a week or so to really dissect this immediate life change. I was 16 years old, numb, insecure and full of fear. Four years had passed with my fear and insecurity ruling my life. I do know that very little was going in a positive direction for me as I was moving through life at a very 'numb' and unfeeling way. Nothing interested me; as a freshman in high school, I failed my AP English class. As a class, we were reading The Great Gatsby, by F. Scott Fitzgerald, and I had been experiencing insomnia as I entered high school. My sleep was in constant disarray and flux as I would have to battle with my father's abuse of alcohol, abuse and infidelity. I was allowed to go to the strip clubs to pick up my inebriated father when he couldn't drive, or bartenders would call to have him picked up. So, thus was the subsequent patterns of my weekends. I went to this science and math magnet program in Austin, Texas. For whatever it is worth, I was not equipped to deal either socially or competitively in the environment with students who were rather ambitious and much more driven than I. I have mentioned that I was deemed 'gifted' at an early age. I still try to meditate and figure what that means, because some of the most impacting people I have met in my life don't have that label or blind ambition, but rather an honest desire to love. This environment that I was injected into was something that I wasn't accustomed to. So that being said, I couldn't sleep, I had an alcoholic father, and Austin was the largest city that I had ever lived in so 'city' life was brand new to me. Needless to say, I was very intimidated and so ill-equipped. I didn't read The Great Gatsby, so I read the cliffs notes and tried to do a paper on it. The English teacher I had at the time, promptly gave me an F. I was entirely crushed. It was the first failing grade I had received in any class what so ever. School was the only place where I derived any kind of validation. In the department of defense schooling systems, I didn't encounter this type of behavior or maybe things just change when you enter high school, but I was academically praised and encouraged in a way that was significantly different than my civilian experience.

Fast forward a year or two, and I managed to pick up my grades to an average C, for this 'gifted' boy that was such a blow to my overinflated ego. My ego was just a childish attempt to try to assert myself in the world. All throughout my educational years and my early adulthood, I was plagued with this insertion of my inflated intellectual pride because I knew I was talented, yet my shame, guilt and fear was crippling my spiritual growth. I was a junior, and in the prior semester I had taken some exam and scored high enough to garner interest from universities and college from across the country. This particular night I had received interest from UCLA and Syracuse. I couldn't believe that I had a choice of the West Coast or East Coast! A little man like me, with potential, and now opportunity. I was enjoying a cigarette in the middle of the night, which was my usual custom as my parents slept, when my dad entered my room. My dad and I had been struggling to connect as much as we could, rather I had been seeking his validation even though he was a very difficult man to live with. Our contentious relationship came to a fork in the road. And years of emotion and resentment brought out the worst in us. In fact, the underlying lack of love and respect came to fruition on this particular night. Again, I was celebrating my minor achievement of just being noticed with a cigarette. See, my father was a smoker as I was. He promptly became an authority figure and in my mind and a hypocrite. What proceeded was a fast and furious argument which then turned into violence. My mother and sister witnessed some behavior that when I reflect on, must seem so traumatic. I have recently spoken with my mother about this incident, and we both agree that it must affect our family with such a negative ripple effect that the damage is still felt the surviving immediate family. My dad and I had our most explosive confrontation yet. It became an abusive barrage of insults and vulgarity, which culminated in violence. My father was choking the life out of me when he threw me up against the hallway and lifted me up with one hand. I could see the hate in his eyes as he called me a fagot as well. Now, this is key because he kicked me out of our home. All my little sister and mother could see was me packing my bag and walking out the door and not returning! As my mom and I discuss this moment of our lives together from different vantage points, she had no idea of what proceeded with the name calling and violence. All my sister and her saw was me abandoning the family.

I packed one bag, and I packed it well with a week's worth of clothes, a bottle of vodka and a pack of smokes. I walked to my best friend's house, whose family had been gracious enough to take me in. I stayed at their house for about two weeks. Let's just say that the bottle of vodka created a schism between that household and I. This traditionally Thai family wasn't accustomed to my antics and lack of control of my drinking. Granted, with hindsight working the way it does, I demonstrated all I knew at that point as far as being an emotional retard (Sorry for insulting the mentally challenged, or anyone with a learning disability. It is a sad state of affairs that I have to apologize for a comment that we all grew up saying in the 80s. However, I can respect others because the respect is given freely for a community to coexist. It is your choice to get offended, but it is my choice to get offended when I'm confronted with things that offend me. It really is my choice on how I react. So forgive me, if I expect the same from you). Drama oh drama, so drama became a new way to cope and intricate part of my life. Drama, both self-created or externally driven and accepted by me, was the fuel that drove my chemical use. Blame also became my MO, and in my mind justifiably so; I can justify just about anything. I was homeless at the age of 16. I burned my bridge at this fine family's home, who had shown me hospitality and compassion. Now, I'm trying to keep high school up and my part time job that was keeping me alive. I was also in a contentious relationship with my high school sweetheart. It was at this point that my Spanish teacher took an interest in me to help me avoid the inevitable, which was dropping out of high school. She opened up her home and let me stay.

I stayed for a couple of weeks trying to maintain a precarious balance between school, relationship, social life and work. At a young impressionable age and a predisposition to chemical abuse, I definitely put an emphasis on my social life. Life as I knew it, took a serious turn for the worse when I decided to drop out of high school and get my GED. Is it entirely possible that there was no other recourse? Sure there is! There is always another way when it comes to the free will that God has given us. The whole point of my journey is to seek and never quit. God doesn't quit on us. In fact, God is love and forgiveness! Hands down, bar none, kick you in the teeth until God gets what is His! Believe in the purpose of the journey for sure! The purpose is love, from Jesus to John Lennon. That is our purpose and faith is knowing that God is real because He manifests Himself in love. That is what I fully believe. That is what the message of Jesus conveys, and I don't believe anyone will argue with the truth of virtues that are expressed in the bible. So, back to the struggle which wages within each and every one of ourselves.

As I can only speak for myself, I am at a point in my life where I am making big grown up decisions, while not possessing the correct perspective or maturity to make the best decision. In other words, I became God, and quit entirely what I had learned and relied on which is Christ's love. An all-encompassing love that incorporates simplicity, hope and forgiveness! I don't believe anyone can argue that these simple themes are the hardest to accomplish in times that demand so much of our time. To stay focused in turmoil, stress, and excessive sensationalism of the human drama, as opposed to the simplicity of what Christ asks is now so clear to me. To me, most movements die when their leader dies. Fact, Jesus existed, fact! Fact number two: The movement is so alive! These are truths that no one can deny. No matter what is argued or doesn't make sense is just a matter of faith. Faith by some definitions is believing is something that you can't apply the five senses. For others it is, having complete trust in something or someone. Yet another definition is a strong belief strong belief in God or a religious doctrine. Simplicity is key, along with acceptance in our own human condition. So, faith is therefore, a necessity that there is always something better. Hope is a byproduct of that belief. If I allow myself to complicate it more and rationalize things I can't explain, then I will be spinning my wheels for the rest of my life. And no real progress would've been made in my personal journey. I would have been stuck, numb, unloving, unruly and joyless. The truth as I understood it as a teenager was about to be put to a decades long test. Trial by trial, by fire, desire, lust, co-dependence and a reluctance to accept the truth which was right in front of my face the whole time. I refused to accept anything any one of faith told me, and went for one heck of a spiritual experiment with no regard for myself. Meaning, I didn't truly know what it meant to truly love myself.

My first real foray into a relationship was that at seventeen with my high school sweetheart. We actually started dating when I was fourteen, as I was now, at sixteen, working full time. I was also living in a roommate situation, and falling in love for the first time in my life with a woman that I would soon get pregnant. I remember the first time I saw her. I will never forget the gold, sparkly flats she wore. It was biology class in high school. She had beautiful brown eyes, and these glasses that just rocked. I guess I have always like the nerdy type. She made me giddy, talk really fast, and just all around sweet. She would write me notes, tell me that she loved me, and we did the normal high school dating things like school dances and movies. I was attention starved and yearning for love like it was the only thing on this planet that could save me, and deep down I knew that it was. We flirted, it was oh so cute. Fourteen and in lust, mistaking it for love. And on some level it was. She was the product of a divorced family, and I was the product of the 'Catholic family staying together for the kids out of duty' (My Catholic brothers and sisters know what I mean). This beautiful young woman was a light that exposed me to my first taste of love and a long-term relationship. My emotional growth at that point wasn't very developed and my insatiable desire for 'love as I understood it' wasn't anywhere near mature enough to handle a new life that we created. Needless to say, our relationship was very contentious as we both struggled with healthy boundaries. I was very sarcastic, temperamental, and I clearly see where my side of the street wasn't clean. I was ill-equipped to deal with a child entering into my life. On March 3, my first daughter was born. Talk about a life changer at the ripe old age of 17! My daughter changed my life for the better. I was there for most of the birthing classes, I read books on parenting and was there at Brackenridge hospital in Austin, Texas, when she was born. I was there to welcome my first child into this beautiful world. This is a moment that is one of my many highlights on my journey. My perception at the time was deeply affected the outcome of this romance. The emotion of love was real. The fear was palpable from both of us though. Insecurity reigned, and I did an almost unforgivable act of leaving the mother of my first child before she was born.

That is such an unforgivable act. One that I will never live down, but is something that I have made peace with many a moon ago. So that being said, I will spend the rest of my life trying to make amends to a young woman, whom I am proud to be a father of. Her mother and I had great times, but they were offset by violent outbursts by a woman who just wanted to be loved like me, who thought we had it in each other at a very young age. That being said, we were not mature enough to raise a child together. At this point, I was scared because she became violent on a few occasions, and with my sarcastic anger disguising an unimaginable pain, made for an impossible relationship. There was no way one knew or understood that hidden sadness and trauma as I understand it now, but back then it was seen as teen angst and an underlying depression that no one could cure or treat. My mother, in her growing frustration with me, started sending me to a counselor, as I had the beginnings of suicidal ideations starting to bud inside of my mind. And throw in physical abuse from a loved one, and my first love, at that! (That is why I ran, my dear child). After almost four years, I walked out of my first long-term relationship. I reflect on the emotion that carried me away from that situation. I feel the need to express deep, deep and haunting regret for my action. Then again, I must also state that it was a stand that I would not subscribe at all to a violent relationship. The same violent tension that I witnessed as a child, and the truth being that I knew there was a better love out there for me. I knew that there had to be more. To this day, I know for a fact that my actions were only looked at from one side, and I am at peace with that. I did nothing to aid my cause, because I was full of fear and guilt over my drinking and selfish lifestyle. There is one thing that sticks out in my mind, and that is that I despised being controlled, or any form of authority, because at that point everything was so negative. I had reached a low point and was turning to the wrong people, places and chemicals for validation and love. It is plain to me that hindsight, working the way it does, in an all-too-familiar light for me. At that time, I led with emotion and heart. That, and that alone, would prove to be a costly way to live. I didn't have any love for myself, none at all. I mean it became all the more difficult when I had to play weekend dad.

First of all, and I don't care what anyone says, visitations are definitely not a relationship. Especially, when you have two different people with two totally different lifestyles. With outlooks on life, spirituality, politics, sexuality, music, religion, temperaments and so on. I mean my first 'love' and I couldn't be any farther apart on things. Because of my unforgivable act of self-preservation, I couldn't get a fair shake in the court of my first 'love's' heart. I mean, to this day, I am not forgiven. Visitations became a will of attrition and scrutiny. Blame was rampant on both sides, and yet I continued to not aid the situation with my depression and use of chemicals. And with no God in my life, things were just a whirling dervish of drama, catastrophe, mayhem, disobedience, drunken outbursts, and unchecked emotions. I was a hellion with a car, a job, independence, and a daughter. I mean seriously? How the heck could I be expected to maintain all of that?

After two years, of this and trying to patch up this on-again-off-again thing with my first baby mama, I was introduced to a new chemical that would forever change my life. Already, my early adulthood was out of the norm, out of control, in huge denial, and extreme intellectual pride. What I mean is, that I was keenly aware that my life up to that point was not like my circle of friends. There was a denial of my inability to cope with drinking and drugs. And finally, there was no way that this 'gifted' student could have done anything wrong. Couple that with an inferiority complex, and there is no reason to fear, right? I had self-assurance that my independence, which I defended tooth and nail, was the 'right' thing. Especially with faith, in nothing but vices at this point. I felt invincible and always right; downright cocky, to be honest. Nothing more than a frightened boy of seventeen with the emotional age of twelve, feeling invincible, not caring about anything makes for one big contradiction (Yes, I'm avoiding what I want to write), so here goes: I used crack cocaine at the age of 19. There is no excuse for this at all, but yet again, I was in this roommate situation, and we were hurting for money and someone had the drunken idea to make some money by making and selling crack. Now, was it curiosity or wanting to be part of the crowd, who knows? All I know was that others experienced something that appeared to be awesome, and I didn't hesitate or think twice about whether or not I should just 'do it' (Sorry, Nike and Britney, oops I did it again!) And after this particular night, I would repeat this action based on instant gratification. 'And only on the weekends!' I would rationalize to myself. My favorite time to indulge was particularly after I dropped off my daughter on the first, third, and fifth weekend of the month. As directed by the great state of Texas. Needless to say, the State of Texas would soon have a greater say in my life. It is only a natural progression, or procession, you be the judge. When I take a look at what my real number one relationship was, it was with chemicals, not my friends, family, or daughter (Sorry Eminem, I don't buy that shit about what your number one relationship is in that song, because it isn't with your daughter. I feel that song is misguided and emboldened a lot of chauvinistic behavior that makes it awfully difficult for men in general to make progress. I have never wanted to kill a woman nor would I ever write a song about it, and call it art. I mean, seriously, what is Bonnie and Clyde about? From what I understand about artistic integrity, it doesn't seem right to work out violence like that and justifying it to children. I feel that we all have a responsibility to others when it comes to children and women.). We live in a society that places more importance on individualism at the expense of community. Now, in this Eminem tangent or rant, I have to express that our nation is experiencing one of the most conflicting times in our history, and I feel it is no coincidence that we have lost our way morally and ethically. I feel I have the right to say this because in my own personal experience, I am entering one of my most Godless parts of my journey; it was one of the most reckless and unloving moments in my young life. And this song is celebrated by the masses, not a family or being with one, but the temerity and celebration of murdering a woman. To write a song about something so deplorable is outright wrong, in my humble opinion. What do we open the door to if we expose our minds and soul to this? My apologies to Marshall Mathers, for his propensity to use shock and awe tactics to sell a record. There is a nuance that should be considered when working out feelings of murder and rage. Music and writing can illicit emotional responses that are so dangerous. My point is that I have felt rage all my life, and I would not give it a second thought to make art like that. Is it because I am a victim of violence and abuse, that a song like that would offend me?

Yet I have no idea as I write about my adulthood. I had no idea how hurt I was, or what I was covering up.

So, I'm sitting at one of my favorite coffee shops in North Austin, thinking about how to proceed with this part of my journey. It seems to me, that the next chapters of my life are so tumultuous, and what I'm carefully trying to do is just avoid all together a glorification of past actions that are at this point in my life, just downright, deplorable. I feel they are pertinent because that was all I knew at that point in my life. I guess that qualifies as a warning or disclaimer. So I enter my twenties as a binge drinker, drug user, and full blown sex addict. At the time I'm OK with that because I feel I earned my stripes to do whatever I wanted. Again, my rebellious nature led me fearlessly through a world that doesn't mind kicking your ass! And believe me, I welcomed all comers, chemicals or not! I held on to my truth and all I believed in, which was literally sex, drugs and rock n' roll, and in that order! Living in Austin Texas at this point has its really good points and attractions. In the early nineties, there was a very vibrant music scene, and I thoroughly enjoyed the free flowing atmosphere of ideas, philosophy, art, music, and of course, chemicals and sex.

As I am sitting here at this wonderful coffeehouse enjoying my Americano and listening to this couple on an obvious first date. They exchanged that nervous and awkward handshake as they talk about obvious generalities and the weather. What strikes me about this encounter is the way in which this is playing out. The woman got here about thirty minutes early, she obviously is trying to contain her excitement, or nervousness. She is dressed very elegantly, her make up is flawless, the attire is casual yet very sexy and she is older and appears to be a little anxious.

Then arrives this younger, very attractive man. The tall, very clean cut appearing male with a few remarkable red flags, according to me! It isn't the fact that I'm bitter and single that I'm examining all of these characteristics, but hear me out, he is wearing shorts and loafers without socks, and tan shorts. Now I ask, is this what qualifies for making a good impression? The woman has obviously put in the time, and the effort this guy could've just as easily gotten out of bed and thrown on these shorts and t shirt. Here goes the conversation: the woman is a private business owner, the man is in real estate but does not have his license, he also states that he is an investor, which to me means he 'flips' real estate, which to me isn't the most stable of work. See, she is enamored by his looks and obvious charm, but is totally ignoring the lack of substance in his opening statement as to why this obvious cluster bomb of a date is just impending doom. Now, I'm not a fortune teller or guru, just an observant man who has learned a lot on my journey.

See, in my early twenties I was a lot like this man, minus the height, haha! Although, I most certainly did have the charm and looks. I had the style and the appearance of being laid back and easy going, while I was anything but. Inside, I was boiling with insecurity, masked by false charm, chemicals, and total denial and unwillingness to look at myself. I put in my headphones because I can't stand to hear this lack of true communication go on. Why do we feel that everything is a show? A presentation, if you will. Now, I'm observing the 'date' with no sound, no verbiage, just body language. She is crossing her legs and moving like she has restless leg syndrome. Meanwhile, he appears to be very engaging, as he appears to be dominating the conversation for the past ten minutes. Very cool! She listened politely and paid acute attention to him discuss various real estate dealings, (I'm totally assuming) but her body language is key to me. She is staring into his eyes, blinking a lot, which to me either she's wearing contacts and her eyes are dry, or she internally doesn't believe half of what she's hearing. This is key to me! She is slumped back in her chair. Her hands flooded politely in her lap, legs uncrossed. Now, I know women well. I think this woman will do the right thing and just use this guy like a douchebag. As the instructions read on most feminine hygiene bottles: Use and discard after use. I say that not out of pride, but out of much experience. I have seen too many women fall for this sort of thing. Have fun, girl! That is what I sincerely hope for (I was essentially raised by my grandmother and mother, and I have experienced much suffering at the hands of the male caretaker that was supposed to nurture me, so I grew up seeing the worst in males). So, I went to get a glass of water to go with my Americano, and I took off my headphones and this conversation has turned into a sales pitch by this guy to this woman about 'investment in real estate.' There are two things to point out about my observation.

I was only half correct about it. One: That the guy was peddling shit and phony, but wrong that it was a date. Or was I? They arrive separately, but leave together. Ha! This makes me think about the lengths we go to conceal or hide what's really going on, for the sake of the presentation or impression. The second point, that I saw and heard is the fact that she told this guy that she had never been here before, but what I had seen was that she knew all the employees here at the shop. They have now driven off in the same direction together. Oh, what a tangled web we weave! From our feelings to our agendas, why do we hide? My point is not whether or not I was correct with my observation, or to even judge. I saw her wedding band. I'm reminded about fidelity and what it means, and I feel awful for just judging the man. How often do we judge without looking at all possible angles?

As I continue to reflect on my life as a young adult, I was all style and absolutely no substance! Much like this young man, I had the sales pitch as to why I was interesting and intelligent. It was when I was nineteen, I got into my second long-term relationship. I had found in my second relationship a musical, sexual and passionate companion; she was nothing like my first love. She shared my love for music, movies, politics and of course, sex! But with these passions that we shared, we lacked the true elements to build a strong relationship. We partied, had copious and passionate sex, and partied in bunches. Her father was a judge here in Austin, and her mother worked for a non-profit organization that does beautiful work in Texas. I mean, I couldn't have asked for a better situation to be in! The conversations were spirited with this woman, and we loved to spend time together. I was faithless, but that didn't matter to me as I was getting my vices met. In the four years that we dated, I hid my number one relationship, which was with sex and chemicals. Moreover, she didn't know that I was abusing drugs. In fact, no one did, from my roommates to coworkers and most of my family, no one knew the extent. Of course, everyone had suspicions and conjectures, but trust me I know all the ways to hide and rationalize. The facade was my specialty. The art of imitation was all I knew, because my only direction at that point was only was to imitate. If you think about it, my learning method was visceral and visual. At that time, I felt it was OK to experience everything I could because all I wanted to do was feel better and what is worst, I felt justified in doing it. I was blind to all whom I hurt, and I didn't care about myself. Nothing more can illustrate this period of my life than all of the bad decisions that I made or subjugated myself to. Now I am being honest and very, very objective about myself, I'm trying to eliminate any justification with these events. Here is where this denial gets downright scary.

To be honest, when you don't give a damn about anything other than vices, life becomes short and meaningless. What made it worse was that I hid it so well, until I caught my first criminal case. It was a minor in possession of alcohol (MIP). My first experience with law enforcement was rather silly and uneventful. I was sitting in the passenger seat of my best friend's car and my older coworker waltzed into the grocery store to get me a six pack of beer. At this time, I had found solace and acceptance from older coworkers and friends. I was always mature for my age, and I found children my age to be trite and immature. Now I reflect on that and really, I was just arrogant; justified by my past hurts and thinking that since I survived them, that I justified in behaving any way I wanted. My friends were awesome, I mean how could they know that they were helping to create a monster. I dated older women, hung out with older men, and all of this at such a young and tender age, believing that I earned my stripes. I never kept in mind all I was taught by my mother or the church. I wanted people to believe that I was amazing, that I had so much to offer, that I was somebody and the places I was going to go (Just like the observation I mentioned earlier). Meaning, that I believed all the bullshit that was being fed to me by the outside world. I had this false belief in myself, I surely did. The circumstances that followed were just absurd, but what do you expect with no God in my life! I just wanted anyone who would listen to know how great I was, what my plans were and how I was so working on making it happen. In the end, I was a lot of passion and commotion, with no substance.

So after this misdemeanor, followed a bizarre string of events, or maybe not so bizarre when chemicals and sex were driving my life. I got another misdemeanor, which was a DUI (driving under the influence). I was a minor so I got five years' probation. I still don't remember the circumstances on that one! All I know is that I got it in 1995. In a total sidebar, I would love to state that not every time I drank or used that I got into trouble, but every time I got into legal trouble, drugs or alcohol was involved. So all the while, I'm in my second long-term relationship with this wonderful woman that had so many similar passions as me. With whom so many good times were shared, but this is one of the most tumultuous times in my life. So of course, I should learn from my mistakes, and I do. I rarely repeat my mistakes, but I continued to drink and use chemicals repeating the insanity of addiction. Here is where my free will just didn't have any real direction, and I was regulated to repeating the same mistakes and paying a legal wage. 1996, was by far my worst year up to that point. I was always on the run from an indescribable pain and trying to fill an unbelievable void in my life. In between parties, awkward social situations and my rebellious nature, I kept on drinking, driving and fornicating. Ahhhh, 1996, well at this point I graduate to a felony crime. It was during my prolific crack use.

One of my weekend entitlements, turned into outright anarchy. I was so unhappy with my career life that was stunted by my own misuse of free will, poor decisions and emotional outbursts. The drinking was not helping at all, I really want to stress that! After my DUI, my girlfriend and I at the time would drink and party incessantly. That led to my third arrest within the span of a year. I was in my early 20s and a store manager at a now defunct retail store. I had the keys, the codes to the alarm and the combination to the safe where all of the money from the registers was kept until the next morning for deposit into the bank.

Earlier in the week, I had been meeting resistance and jealousy from other coworkers and my superiors. I was not a happy camper with this current relationship or my job position in life. I was 'gifted!' Damn, I deserved better; I am better than this, and no one understands me! The anger that was within, came to the surface. I couldn't contain it any longer. I was just placed on another probation the month prior because I was charged with assault with my current girlfriend at the time (yes, the one whose father was a judge). Man, I was both stupid and blind. Mostly, I had let my ego run amok. To me, I have a series of acronyms that help me remember things because I have a tendency to be such a knucklehead. To me, EGO stands for 'edging God out.' Amen? Every time I take the wheel, it doesn't go well for me. I would make an awful captain of a ship because there was definitely not a strong enough wind to carry my sails. That is what life without God is for me, for sure! So here it is, one of the most egregious misuses of free will. I walked into my store, with my Rage Against the Machine T-shirt (I'm so sorry to misrepresent you guys). And I just waltz into the store, unlock the gates, unlock the safe, grab $15,000 and waltz right out the front door, in front of the janitor (who was a good friend, I do stress was), and straight into my car. I won't go into details as to what transpired afterward for the next few days. Literally, that is all it lasted. Did I make an investment? Did I make any philanthropic contributions, HELL NO! I was in ultimate abuse mode, and didn't care how badly I hurt myself or my future. If I was pissed off about my status as a human being, well I sure as shit didn't help myself out. So at this point, I return to my parent's home in Lockhart, Texas. I was crashing something sort of awful. I mean, when you get so high you come down really hard, emotionally and physically. This child of God, this boy trapped in a man's body, was definitely not my mother's son. I sure as hell was not a good son, but God saw fit to meet me where I was at. Hear me out! (Please)

So, I had been battling depression since I was a child; I had been to therapy with suicidal ideations and counseling. There is nothing worse for depression than the amount of chemicals and false validations, than the come down! Withdrawal from alcohol or drug for me was a constant derision of inner chatter that made me so small. From extreme elation of emotion bliss that comes crashing down to an emotional pit of hell. Tears, guilt, the hurt in my mother's eyes, all dragging me into a withered version of whom I was the night before. It was awful! I couldn't bare the guilt of what I had done. I knew I was in deep trouble. My employers were calling my house phone. The district manager was leaving me messages along with loss prevention and the store manager. I mean, there must have been at least 20 messages on the machine as I struggled to gain some sort of sanity. My lack of faith in salvation led to one of my few regrets in my life, but yet one of the most valid conversions in my struggle to find peace and sanity. As I mentioned, I was at my parent's home. They were at work in Austin, Texas (Now I have been struggling to find good things about my father as he passed back in February, and this is one of the few); I knew where my father kept his guns. I promptly loaded a shotgun and a .38 special. I couldn't take another condescending voicemail, or at least my ego couldn't. I mean, don't they know who I think I am? I made three phone calls. My last one was to my dad, and I'm not exactly sure how much time passed between the phone call and my placing that gun to my head, but my dad literally made the drive from Austin to Lockhart in about 20 minutes! This is one saving grace that I'm so grateful to my father for. He was always quick to discern when danger was lurking or when to act. I'm a lot like him in that regard, along with his temper. In the time that I had loaded the weapons and held that .38 firmly to my head, like an angel, he appeared and calmly removed the gun from my hand. He essentially saved my life and for that I'm eternally grateful. Thanks dad! What a rude introduction to my twenties that I brought that upon myself with a crime for the ages, what a way to usher in adulthood.

What follows is just a repeated pattern of chemical use, misfortunes, and now hospital stays and medication. Along with that, is the stigma of being diagnosed with a mental illness, medications that robbed me of my best and coupled with total self-doubt. I still had no God in my life, or at least not an active prayer life, or discipline. My four year relationship that had been based on vices and basic passions came to an end, as her family encouraged her to leave me. I had no argument or objection, I was in no way a good boyfriend. My second long-term relationship ended with infidelity and much pain that kept me astray. But my yearning for love and comfort kept me going back to the streets and my precious vices with my weekend rewards to myself, for the stripes I felt I earned, and self-pity that I lavished on myself like my own personal manna.

Unfortunately, I repeated this pattern of falling in and out of love, quitting or getting fired from jobs, and false lies that I kept spewing in that fruitless mind talk. I literally fell for everything because I believed in nothing. I don't think I went but a few months without having someone to either sleep with or do my chemicals with. I was rarely alone or in solitude with God, except to pray to get me out of trouble. I didn't have the proper prayer life, and that is my truth at that point in my life. The beauty of this life for me is the acceptance of my mistakes and suffering. That has been one of my strongest characteristics, along with my love of truth. I have been honest with my faults to the point that I now display my weakness for all to see. Yes, that is a hard way to live, but to be perfectly honest I live a way more independent and spirited life. Although, many don't see it that way, to me the truth has set me free. To the point so that

I'm not burdened and that has totally expanded my faith. Please follow me here, there is so much more to tell!

After committing my first felony, breaking a tenuous probation that my rebelliousness brought upon myself and my addiction to chemicals, I underwent a different kind of journey into mental health. A new kind of chemical dependence if you will. One that was as detrimental to my physical well-being as any chemical I've ever tried. Seeing how this is probably one of the most insidious and false dependencies I have ever encountered, it was one of the most unproductive periods of my life. With the lack of direction, spiritually, I again was left to my vices and self-made solutions to age old problems. In this modern day of technological advances, beautiful materials, fast cars that don't last as long as the Chevys I grew up with, the age old solution is faith. What has been the one constant since Christ's death? There must be some truth because it has lasted for over 2,000 years! I will keep emphasizing my misuse of my free will and my misplaced beliefs in myself. That would keep me hidden from what is obvious truth to most, an absolute veil of darkness from my bad choices. With death lurking at every turn and fear still dictating my actions, I finally turned to medicine to help me cope with my internal battle. It was around this time I entered the rooms of recovery meetings, went to group therapy, and individual counseling. My foray into this modes of coping were helpful to a point. I saw their purpose, but to me it wasn't a complete solution. How is it that these are the only options available in this land of plenty? Was I completely honest? NO! Did I make use of all of my supports? No! To my credit, I did educate myself and participate in the program, even if I didn't exactly know what I was doing. There isn't a road map for all of this. I'm not perfect and neither is anyone, 'let he without sin…cast the first stone!' (I don't think I need to give a footnote here! Truth was spoken.) My point is that is an arduous journey if not taken seriously, and I was in my early twenties without money or adequate health insurance. Thanks to that most special recovery group though, I started to try to understand what humility was, or at least I began to search within myself as to the root of the problem. In my earliest attempts at self-discovery, there was a constant struggle to get past the surface drama, past hurts and of course, chemical dependency, all of which, without any spiritual direction and misplaced faith. I again tried all I could as far as prescribed medicine, spilling my problems to anyone who would listen, and all the while clinging onto my vices.

Here is a quick rundown of my life at 23. I had a daughter, I'm a convicted felon, I'm addicted to all vices external, I'm very self-centered, individualistic, I'm driving a brand new car (a 1994 Mitsubishi Eclipse, which was a nice sports car!), I had been through two long-term relationships totaling about eight years of my life, I had a serious attempt at suicide, I had my independence since I was 16 years old, and no God whatsoever in my life! Since my life had no substantial faith, my life back then was focused on the insidious cycle of keeping it all together. The rent, the car payment, the social life, the child support and relationships. It is Socrates, the father of philosophy that embarked on a simple premise, 'know thy self.'

It was so hard to look at myself while I was so busy trying to fill insatiable desires and voids in my life. Can anyone feel me on that? How do I profess to love others, if I don't care and love myself? I kept putting myself in the most absurd situations, circumstances and relationships. Seeking a solution in the exterior, never taking the time to figure out what made me happy in the first place. Add to that the dangers of putting myself out there like that. It is a total blessing that I am not dead, or that I didn't kill anyone on the road as I was quite inebriated a lot of times behind the wheel. Looking back on all of these situations, there is a lot to be thankful. In the years 1996–2000, I was arrested at least ten times, and convicted on about eight of them. What could possibly make me be thankful for things like that? If hindsight is 20/20, then self-discovery has to start somewhere, right? It was in the rooms of recovery that I feel I began at least to start. Chemicals were beginning to bring me to my knees and damn near killing me, but I was too wrapped up in the wrong kind of selfishness to see a way out.

Another job, another long-term-relationship wasted and now the tightrope of probation while balancing all my vices. There is a stone cold truth here, as I went from relationship to relationship seeking love and validation; I'm a decent looking guy, intelligent, independent, and the life of the party. This is how others knew me, all the while, I'm weak on the inside and on the road to eternal death for sure! Eternal death isn't that fire and brimstone bullshit. All I do know is that in this life, we have just this moment, and we share it with one consciousness being united in what people in the program call a God consciousness. Is religion or recovery the whole answer? Probably not. To be completely honest, I have felt that Karl Marx's famous quote about religion is only half right. I feel that opium is the opium of the masses. I have always felt that just reliance on doctrine alone gets people nowhere, just ask any communist or nihilist. I mean, all work and no play…makes for dull, dull, living. That being said, burning the candle at both ends makes for a very short life. Ask any of my rock idols: Jimi Hendrix, Janis Joplin, and Jim Morrison etc.…(Yes, I'm that old) How do I break this cycle to avoid an early grave like them and many others?

As I mentioned before, recovery groups were my beginning of searching inward. The 12 steps have a lot of truth to them. The men that started this journey out of total and complete demoralization knew that their experiences were valuable and community vital to recovery. Believe me, I felt every bit of that pressure. To gain a rebirth in this life, I had to learn to appreciate the moment or life would just pass me by. I guess one of my many fears was to wake up at 90 and realize that life had done exactly that, passed me by. I sure as hell don't want to experience that! I have seen many people live miserable lives. All we have is this moment, and if we miss out on it that would be eternal death. I love that section in the third step that says, "God as we understood Him." I love that, because that was all I could see at the time. Chemicals were drowning my spiritual life. Quashing my will to live and that is ever so dangerous for a child of God (I don't care what your dogma is, the human spirit is getting smashed to bits more and more these days). I still had so much work to do and I understood that, but when my willingness is being diluted by vices I so struggled to hang on, it made for a very miserable and contradicting life. I struggled with my use of chemicals for sure, but in recovery they are 100% correct; it is a spiritual malady. That is why the initial ideas and truths that were started in the early 1930s have endured for so long and have spawned over 200 different groups that deal with everything from alcohol to overeating. The beauty of this program is the honesty, willingness and open-mindedness that are required to be successful. What I have done is apply it to my faith, and the results have been astounding! My life is testament of being open-minded and willing to work through every circumstance that was presented before me. I am eternally grateful to the men and women that helped guide me and mold me in the rooms of recovery.

Now as a very important sidebar, I injured my back one February day in 1998. I was helping my parents move into their brand new home in Lockhart, Texas. I was lifting a cabinet off of the bed of a pick-up truck, and I ended up tearing a disk in my back in the lumbar spine. The L1-S5 to be exact. This begins my battle with chronic pain, and yet another introduction to a new family of prescribed medicine (Vicodin and all of its insidious companions). I was 23 at the time and looking back at the whole situation, I should've dropped the damn thing! I have had multiple back surgeries, numerous trips to pain centers and physical therapy. With doctors and prescription pills feeding this monster. Not to mention my dollars feeding a more corrupt monster.

As I entered my third attempt at a long-term relationship, I was coming to realize a lot about myself. I felt I was growing and making progress. But again, my vices would continue to haunt me. 1999 was a very difficult time for me. I had entered another relationship that would encompass a few more years of my life, and during this time would complicate my already complicated life, but not in the sense that most would consider bad. As I mentioned earlier, I was on probation for a felony and a number of misdemeanors. I'm living a very fearful existence, while hiding every aspect of my weaknesses such as probation, recovery meetings and therapy. I still had no active prayer life other than the common, "God, please get me out of…(insert circumstance here)." And a blind vanity about myself, that somehow, I was doing great! It may be obvious to most what was lacking in my life. I have always been a mercurial spirit, a student of life and a compassionate soul, which have always been my saving graces. We all have a saving grace that makes us a redeemable light and that is love and acceptance, not just of others but of ourselves being citizens of this beautiful planet. I live with great passion, and I have always had a big heart. So my precarious balancing act would get me a wake-up call that forced an instant self-examination. One could say that it was forced, or others may say that I got what I deserved, but I am truly grateful for the circumstances that followed.

After the dissolution of my second long-term relationship, while I was on probation, I took two hits of a marijuana joint. I was in total self-pity mode and blaming myself for the break up. But ten days later, I had to report to probation and I pissed dirty. That reckless devil of feeling sorry for myself came up to bite me in the ass. I knew I would come up dirty. The real question is whether I loved myself enough to care! Almost as quickly as I had inhaled, the state of Texas revoked my tenuous probation. I ended up serving most of 1999 at the Del Valle Correctional facility, located just outside of Austin, Texas. What a way to welcome my third long-term relationship with a wonderful soul, who just didn't understand the type of man she was involved with. Hell, I didn't even understand myself, as I was just beginning that journey myself. I'm not even 25, and my life is entering this sort of Darwinian nightmare, in an environment where only the strong survive. I had no idea what to expect, but let me preface this by saying I wouldn't wish any type of incarceration on my worst enemy. Absolutely nothing can prepare you for what goes on in there. I don't care how tough or gangster anyone believes that they are. As for me, I didn't give a shit because I didn't have much self-worth, and I was equally naive. So, I had both of those characteristics working for me. I am a man that stands at 5'6" tall on a good day with Doc Martens on. At the time, I weighed about 140, I'm fairly lean. I'm not the most masculine man that walks the face of the earth, and I love sex almost as much as I loved chemicals at the time. It's crazy how readily both are easily available at the Travis County Correctional Complex (TCCC). I don't believe I entered the facility with any fear of it. Thank God, because I wouldn't have reacted so fearlessly, or with grace, because what ensues is almost unbelievable.

It was early spring 1999, and I had to turn myself in for my violations of my multiple probations. The moment I entered this enormous building which housed about one hundred or so inmates, I felt like I was being watched. What I received the following months of my incarceration was a rude introduction to the prison gang life. I entered the crowded phone booth to make my initial phone call to let my parents and girlfriend know that I had finally made it. I felt the stares of multiple eyes on me. Try to envision that scene in Shawshank Redemption, where Tim Robbin's character was walking into prison, and I was immediately shoved in the chest like a hockey cross check by a man who I became my cellmate. Looking back on it now, I know it was a sign to others. The first night was tough, but I had already been in custody for about a month anyway as I was arrested in another county for driving with a suspended license. As I was exhausted from my transfer between different counties, I endured this man's story about how he had been in prison for ten years and was released on parole and had only been out for two weeks. In his two week sip of freedom, this man violated his parole, committed more crimes and was heading back to prison. Each night he would tell me about his story. And I was so naive as to what he was getting at, but this event haunts me to this day. The third night of my new environment was literally hell.

That third night, he pulled his pants down and was fully erect. It was fight or flight for my body. I didn't have time to think, I was so scared, but I moved with grace. I defended my body. The following day I had him transferred to a different cell, but with grace I knew I couldn't have this man lose face in front of his friends. He was clearly institutionalized and that is his truth. But this is my body, and I had to learn how to physically fight. What ensued the following weeks and months was a constant fight (physical and otherwise). I will mention that he was a part of a prison gang and let's just say I was blessed to fight and take physical punishment. One of the fruits of that experience is that I learned to defend myself and control my fear. During my many months there, I learned that I was being put through what is known as a 'heart check.' It is true that I have heart, but I also know that I have never been one to join the crowd, and I wasn't about to start there. Fear was a constant for me throughout my life, but I became so accustomed to it that I finally learned to control it. I earned a lot of respect for not running and standing up for myself, all the while not spreading what this guy tried to do to me. It was a precarious position to be in, but we all know what happens to snitches in jail. It's the code not only in jail, but on the streets for sure! If you think about it, it's the code for even police and the 'good ole boy' network all over this country. From gangs, to religion secrecy, has permeated throughout. And to me, that is bullshit. I'm not comfortable with the secrecy. I don't like it, but I'm a man of my word these days and I won't talk about it. Like other things in my jail story. But it's all true. I'm a man of love and this was the last time I actually fought back and hit someone. I hate violence, that is true. I'm a lover not a fighter, but when it's my body, there is a different gear that kicks in and I had to defend myself and my honor.

This is a very precarious time for me. Jail is an experience I wouldn't desire to befall anyone, not even my worst enemy. Not only was it a dangerous place, a place that breeds a culture that stifles all hope, but an environment that truly only the strong survive and a strength is the sole means of survival. So, I understand the fear driven societies of gangs in general. I get it, one of my uncles is in a gang. I've seen it on the streets firsthand. I can see where a person finds him or herself a slave to a lifestyle and mentality where the only way to live is to be incarcerated. I saw firsthand what the fruits of recidivism bare. It is a lie driven by fear, so hard to conquer that it leads to an infinite cycle of crime and false security. There isn't a day that goes by that I don't think of this pivotal moment in my life, and I reflect with gratitude, not pride like I used to, about how I overcame my fears. This is a fact that resonates with me to this day. It was the last time I ever hit someone back.

I am in reflection and a search for things that my dad did right in my life while he was alive, and they are few and far between. I wrote him a letter while I was in jail explaining to him what happened, and that if I was hurt or killed, I named the names of the men who were involved. Curiously, to me, he didn't respond. When I was done serving my time, he was the one that picked me up. Again, in a moment when I needed him, he said nothing. I cried the whole way home in the car. To him, every time I cried, it was weak. It was one of those awkward moments where he and I didn't talk when I needed direction. He always looked down on me for being emotional or sensitive. As we were driving along Highway 183 toward Lockhart, I saw a church on the side of the road that caught my eye. I asked my dad to pull over so I could pray. I mentioned earlier how there was strength in numbers, I would pray with men every night before I went to bed. It was a small group of about 15 men that would circle up and pray each night. We ministered to each other and drew strength from each other. It was led by a blessed African American man whom I looked up to in there. I know what you're thinking, jailhouse religion! The cold hard truth is that in a dire circumstance like jail, only fifteen out of about one hundred men banded together. That is a small number of men if you do the math, and I went through the entire ridicule of other men in the jail expressing their displeasure with us hypocrites. What is hypocritical about praying when one is in dire straits? Hasn't faith and prayer always been ridiculed and discounted, though? Aye, there is the rub, even on the outside of jail walls, prayer has been reduced to wishing someone well, like a greeting a passerby on the sidewalk of a big city.

It is true, I had seen the light! I wanted to go into this Catholic house of worship and pray. I wanted to continue and expand my prayer life. I was going to implement all the changes I meditated on in jail. I was a changed man! Instead, the chapel was locked and I couldn't get in. But outside was a beautiful statue of our blessed Virgin Mary. So, outside in front of my dad, I knelt and wept like a baby beside this statue, as my dad turned his back. This will have to qualify as a good moment as my dad allowed me to do this. For me, it was growth, because it was the first time I turned to Mother Mary for guidance and intercession. Well, I didn't know that at the time that that was what I was doing, but it is exactly what I was doing. It was the beginning of learning to surrender which is oh so difficult in this life. I must say that I am grateful to my dad for allowing me to do this. I am grateful to my dad for allowing God to be a part of my family, even though for whatever reasons only known to God and him, my father was never really religious or did he go to church on a regular basis. So his heart couldn't have been all bad, or evil. I was not yet 25 years old.

This is the point in my journey, that I will pause with my misadventures to state that prayer is so important in my life and how I have since that time in front of that statue of Our Lady of Fatima, that I was humble enough to really hit my knees in despair. It took a quarter century of living to begin to examine prayer or the possibility of what humility could mean in my life. The mere act of kneeling was such a foreign concept to me. I mean literally almost a full year of being incarcerated, would bring anyone to their knees. But that's just it! Why does it take total despair to bring me to God? Again, this is my journey up to this point. I'm questioning everything from love to my own existence; I'm almost 25 and just starting to learn how to pray. My prayer life is oh so different today. So, let me first state that the first thing I did was hit my knees in total supplication, with lowered head. And I was oh so grateful for being alive, not being raped, and now I was physically free from jail. Here is a very important illustration about prayer; my father always said that he prayed to God. Although, he would not go to church on a regular basis, nor was he present as a father. He would always state with a great deal of emphasis that he prayed. Although, the fruits of his prayer weren't evident; his constant criticism, anger and negativity would permeate like a cancer throughout the household on a daily basis. By contrast, my life consists of a prayer life that continues to grow on a daily basis, and my disposition is vastly differs than that of my father's at the time. I knew he resented that fact in myself. Like the bitterness of the other men in jail, at the sight of fifteen men praying together, my father was bitter that I would always choose a different path than him. Alas, I found a way to be grateful to him, as my father allowed me to explore this avenue of faith.

There are five forms of prayer that are written about in the Catholic faith, they are: Blessing, intercession, petition, thanksgiving and praise. Now, keep in mind that I'm not a priest, saint or holy man. I'm just a man on a journey, one who has had a childlike questioning of everything. I feel, and I can only speak for me, that everyone is on this search, from Jew to Gentile. And I believe, if I keep it simple in those terms that means everyone on this planet, regardless of religious affiliation, has a moral compass that gives us all hope. I say this with supreme confidence because I have been to all sorts of temples and prayed searching for answers. Form mosque, to temple to church, I have prayed with many different denominations. Prayer is the uniting bond of us all that comforts the struggle within ourselves and gives us grace. At first, I was so limited in my prayers, because I was so concerned with, 'Am I doing it right?' I was confined by dogma and religion which some people were so instant on getting it exactly correct. Since the ripe old age of five, I had been rebelling against it in Omaha, NE. The whole discipline was foreign to me. I had no idea where to start. I had an idea, but no direction, but it all starts at home. Since the head of household didn't even take time to show me how to be a man, he didn't pray or at least not that I ever saw him. I had no idea where to start. All I knew, was that desperation and suffering made me do it. So, as it stands in the current state of affairs in the world, Houston, most of the Gulf Coast and Central Texas has been hit by hurricane Harvey. It will go down as one of the most expensive and devastating natural disasters in modern history, and as with all the suffering in my life, most of the nation has been driven to prayer out of desperation and despair. So, I'm not alone in being driven to desperation; I believe America was a divinely inspired country. Why else would we subscribe to tolerance, certain freedoms and justice? Regardless of political ideology that has polarized us into factions of hate and mistrust? Are we not the hope of millions of people around the world? At this very moment, we are a country lacking a just leader (I won't get into politics, although the temptation is great at the moment. I studied political science at Texas State University for a brief time). I mean I don't care what your dogma or politics is, we are a nation under God, aren't we? To me, this is why we suffer; our lack of charity, which is love. God is love isn't he? John Lennon said it best: "All You Need is Love!" Amen? I must always keep things simple, therefore, if I lose my sense for the common good, don't the ones I love suffer most?

Like my household, my leader was absent, so my mom had to take the reins and try to do it all spiritually. She tried to instill prayer in my life, but I was so rebellious that I refused. It took almost 25 years to literally get me on my knees. I started this story out with the emphasis on free will, God gave me this choice to either accept the tools given to me or make the choices to get me where would lead me to this simple truth: PRAY. Now, what's the use? One may ask. I pray and nothing happens? Or, I don't do it right. I mean, in this world so full of choices, I made the choices to try everything but, obedience and reverence for God! In this commercially driven society with so much choice in this land of plenty, what do we really crave? As I can only speak for myself, I think of the times that I was most desperate, and since this little epiphany of hitting my knees that was enforced upon me out of desperation, I know I'm not the only one praying at this moment. So, this brings me back to my search. And for what? LOVE! I needed it more than ever. So, I returned to this relationship with a woman who introduced me and fed my need for love as I understood it at the time, which was sex. This wonderful passionate woman was bisexual, was Swedish, had a very open mind and just as hypersexual as I was. She loved me, she stood by me while I was incarcerated and indulged my appetite for this craving that I only knew to satiate with sex. Keep in mind, that I'm still self-soothing myself sexually (masturbation) and having copious sex with her. I also battled chemical abuse as well as still maintaining my faith in the world.

Fresh out of jail, I was entering the winter of 1999, and facing the new year. Y2K, if memory serves correctly. There was a concern, if not a panic in some circles that there would be some sort of computer shut down and computer systems couldn't calculate the change in year. I was still just happy to be free, I actually slept straight through it; I was truly appreciating a soft bed. I entered 2000 with a newfound sobriety, a focus on meetings and a growing yearning for community. On January 6 2000, I joined AmeriCorps to help my growing yearning for community, with the lofty ideals of doing some good. I had always been civic-minded and very passionate about politics, and I've always been concerned about the poor. So this seemed as the best possible way to contribute, and quite frankly, to change my negative effect. I also gave my time to help the homeless, yet to my detriment again, I was on such fragile ground. I was in such doubt about myself, and I was still clinging to a world of emotional outbursts, which I felt were justified. As I mentioned, I was dating a very free woman who expanded my mind and my body. Intellectually speaking, she and I had very agreeable dispositions and similar political views, and very high sex drives. Up to that point, I'm still clinging onto vices and the external views of love. Like I was on a perpetual dating game, and the good life consisted of all these generalities like: 'What's your sign?' And 'What is a nice girl like you, doing in a place like this?' I mean, I fully believe now that you get what you give. I'm living life like a true bohemian. Art, music, philosophy, sex, drugs, multiple sex partners and many drunken nights. Monogamy was some archaic practice for squares! I was so enlightened. I was the man! I had accomplished the dream! Strip clubs, group sex, lust, gluttonous behaviors, and my being so defined and independent. Oh, and did I mention I was tutoring youngsters for their GEDs and building homes in the poorest parts of Austin? I was making a difference (Yes, totally sarcastic). For every soul I thought I helped, my spiritual life was totally empty. For all I thought I was so happy, I was dead. I had no clue what true joy was or my life would have been more fulfilling.

I was the living reincarnation of a Dionysian wannabe, living life to the fullest. I was never looking back, and only living in the moment. Carpe diem right, but like the theater celebrated version life of Dionysus, my life was still such a drama. I'm like an unknown Jim Morrison, burning the candle at both ends and convincing myself that was a true way to live. My actual truth at the time was, whom was I serving? With all my 'good' works and self-serving compassion, it seems to me that my generosity was misguided. That it may have been self-serving to justify my lifestyle. Now, that is a very harsh criticism of myself, or is it? What I am saying here is that I was very self-centered. I wasn't truly a giving person, and that made me disingenuous. This reminds of some writings from one of the doctors of our faith, named St. Teresa of Avila, who wrote about false humility. She wrote about how she liked it when her spiritual advisor would find fault with her. So if my whole search has been to find truth, fight cynicism, and be a good person, then my good works were shallow if I was doing these good works without any consideration of the state of my soul. Believe me, I wasn't at all concerned with my soul's state of being. According to the things she had written about I did things with the best intentions, but I was living a lie, to myself, so to me it is no surprise that my personal demons would come back to haunt me. It is the perfect illustration of false humility.

So, to illustrate my point, I reflect back on the misguided good intentions that I had, and of course, the self-serving nature that I used to justify my denial of the truths that I had been rebelling from since my early elementary encounters. My first mistake was my choice of living situation. I had rented a home in East Austin, which at the time before it was gentrified, was riddled with drugs and prostitutes. For a man who was trying to get those demons off his back, it was a totally logical choice. My second mistake was in a choice of a roommate, as I would come to find out was a recovering heroin addict. I chose this place for obvious reasons, because it was close to work and cheap. Also, under the misplaced notion that I was doing civic-minded work and giving back to the community. Now, I bought the whole line of self-delusion and my own personal bullshit. I was matching my intentions with action for the first time in my life, and to some extent it was very, very rewarding. There is story after story of great work done by a wonderful program that served the community. In an ideal world, if all it took was civic duty and good intentions then my soul would be saved, and all would be right as rain, and the communists, without God or sin, would rule the world. Although, I'm sure even God has love for a communist!

My new found sobriety, roommate, and living situation lasted about 8 months, and the demons of crack and sex pervaded my life, yet again. I remember the two key events that brought me and my scheme down in spectacular fashion. The first event was my roommate, whom one night crawled into bed with me. She was naked and felt wonderful in bed. There was no sex, no sexuality all together, but the longing for companionship took hold. I realized how lonely I was. The second event also involved my roomie, and it was that I discovered the fact that she was abusing heroin, and I found her on the steps of our house under the influence. Needless to say, it was just a matter of time before I was off to my own personal race of addictions and temporary solutions. The emptying vacuum of pleasures that just eight months prior had scared me straight. Just eight months prior, I had spent it incarcerated and was ready to throw it all away. All to fill a void that was unfillable Being human and free became a spiral to death, and God gave me the will to choose this, or accept the truth. I left my noble cause because it just couldn't pay the bills, and the location was a 'danger' to my sobriety, or at least that is what I told family and friends. My true motive was that I needed more money for drugs and partying. I started working at a clinic, and got an apartment in South Austin. Oh my! What nobility and lack of providence on my part.

Who was I serving? It sure wasn't the poor or the disadvantaged. And I most definitely wasn't serving God. Just when I thought I couldn't get any lower, or feel any emptier, I kept on with the old ways and lies. My humility experiment turned into a vanity project to protect and hide my selfishness, hence St. Teresa of Avila was a spot on description of my deception of self. I was a true depiction of false humility.

I started to work in the medical field again. Thus, turning to what I had known since I was sixteen. The life of spinning my wheels paycheck after paycheck, thinking that if I worked harder my life would improve. The more I felt that I was making progress, the more toxic I became. Within a matter of months, I was back in full party-sex mode. I am in a place where I was older, wiser and again invincible, which led me to dark places. Further and further I fell into darkness and sin. My life revolved around that circular figure eight of insanity without an end in sight, much like a hamster in a wheel. It felt like every payday was this cycle of getting paid, recovering from the party then struggling through the week until the next paycheck. And why not? I was single (after another failed relationship with that beautiful Swedish woman), decent looking, fairly intelligent and the life of the party!

At this point, I met a woman who, at the time, was very inspirational to me finding something 'real' as far as a relationship. I am grateful to this woman for many things, as she saved my life in more ways than one. I remember the first time I saw her, she looked like a ray of light with the most classic smile I had ever seen in my life. She was applying for the vacant provider position with the medical director of our clinic. Our community clinic was serving the uninsured in Austin. She was dressed professionally and had a very sophisticated and elegant look. I knew we were looking for a physician assistant, and I was intrigued from the moment I saw her. As luck would have it, she made a very good impression and was hired for our practice. Within a week or so, we had begun conversing. What a pleasure to find out that she was Catholic, and just a year or two younger than me. We had a lot in common, we were both intelligent, likeminded, similar political ideologies, and she liked my positivity and energy. What I loved most was that she believed in me. She made me feel more confident in myself. People would look at us, and it was like we owned the room. And to top it off, we started to go to church together and praying the rosary. For the first time in my life, I dated a Catholic woman and was actually not interested in sex. Don't get me wrong, she was an elegant and very attractive woman, but more importantly, we didn't sleep together. For the first time in my life, I felt a love I had never known before; a relationship not based on sex. Let me be very clear, there was a very strong mutual attraction. But at this point in our journeys, we were searching for something deeper. We had both had enough of the secular dating scene, and we were both getting over long-term relationships that didn't benefit us in anyway.

We dated for about six months, but we never became intimate. That was so new to me. In fact, this was a foreign concept to both of us. We explored the spiritual side of a chaste relationship as prescribed by the Catholic Church. For both of us, this was just something real and fulfilling. So my conundrum during those six months was this: I hadn't revealed my darkest secrets to her, meaning, my vices and addictions. To her, I was sort of like a spiritual guru or sage and noble man. And for six months, I was totally that! I grew in wisdom and clarity. Not to mention, that I was totally clean and sober for six months. I put a ton of faith in this relationship. She was my saving grace (the one). One night, we discussed the possibility of getting married. She was making great money and paid me one of the greatest compliments I had ever received in my life. She wanted to put me through school. She wanted to pay for it all. She loved my mind. She thought it was a waste for me to be working in medical administration. So, about a week or so later, we went out for drinks after work at a Mexican restaurant in South Austin that was very close to my apartment. It was a very fun night, we went out with coworkers and it was a total blast. We got lit. It was the first time that we got totally drunk. I mean sloppy drunk. So much so, that we skipped the check, and took a cab to my apartment.

The usual drunken buffoonery was about to ensue. Now after many margaritas and six months of abstaining from sex, the proverbial escapade was actually taking place. The passionate, lust driven, emotional, and is taking place in my living room. Now as far as couples like us go…it should be wonderful, sensual, loving, like couples are supposed to experience for the first time, right? Especially a loving couple who had visions of marriage, kids and the whole nine yards. The attempt at our first intimate encounter was anything but the aforementioned ideal. It was sloppy; lust. For us, whom had had experienced the act of intimacy in our pasts, it was awful. I remember her being aggressive and me not being able to perform. In laymen's terms, I couldn't get it up. We both passed out, undressed and unsatisfied. I awoke at about three or four in the morning. And the song 'clocks' by Coldplay was on repeat and at a very loud volume. I remember being frustrated by my lack of performance and irritated that she was naked on the bed. There was always a part of me, after all of these years, that reflects on this action every day of my life. This is where I encounter God in my life.

I made the decision to go out and use. I went on a three day drug binge. All of my insecurities and secrets were there for the world to see. I commenced on my usual disappearing act. My self-centered pain that only the external could cure. It was like a little boy who only knew one way of coping and dealing with things, the chemical solution to spiritual problems. I hold myself to a very high standard. I still do that to this day. I expected a lot of myself, I relied on this woman to 'save' me. I put all my faith in her. And as I delved into my usual solution, I plummeted back into that empty, hateful depression that almost killed me in 1996. The old familiar sharks could smell the blood in my ocean of self-delusion and lack of self-worth. I bore the brunt of the responsibility for this action. The truth is, I felt ashamed, unloved and accountable to the point of again committing the ultimate sin in God's eyes. I put my faith in a woman. And I surely did let her and her family down. The demons that I tried so hard to hide had forced their way out of me like a volcanic mountain that had no way of preventing the eruption of hate that I felt for myself for being weak (yet again).

It was March 19 2003, I missed work, I hadn't talked to anyone and people that loved me were frantically searching for me. For my lover at the time and her family, it was beyond their comprehension of what was unravelling before their eyes. A total deconstruction of a man that in their eyes, was going to marry their oldest daughter. After my three day disappearing act, a few observations on my personal destruction are the distinct differences between my family and her family's reactions. To my mother and father this was old hat. My disappearing act was second nature. They actually didn't do anything or show any concern. My prospective family actually panicked and called every hospital, every shelter and public authority. They were actually driving around looking for me for three days! They never would have found me. Even my employer, whom had been very supportive of me, and quite frankly loved me, tried searching for me. I was in my own personal hell feeling extreme hate of myself for this pain I couldn't overcome. My pain was so overwhelming that my coping mechanisms only gave me temporary relief. I literally couldn't feel anything. This pain that had been hounding me since my childhood came to head. With my last money, I bought my chemical of choice and felt nothing. I took a taxi home and had the final solution to my pain. The contrast between people that raised me and people that wanted to love me was clear. It is the perfect difference between health and dysfunction. The reactions I can hold myself accountable to are that I had a clear choice, and that was life or death. And quite frankly, I didn't care about either. I may never had to this point in my life.

I got to my apartment in South Austin at some point during the day, which made the date March 23, when I finally ran out of money, drugs and courage. I entered my apartment alone and noticed that my belongings had been searched through; I guess my girlfriend took the express liberty to go through my things. Quite frankly, I couldn't blame her. I couldn't feel anything, like a Nine Inch Nails song, "There is no you, there is ONLY me!" During my 45 minute or so taxi ride, that I had bounced a personal check to pay for, I wept during the whole ride. That was the first time I had wept with wailing cries and guttural runts. I knew that I had but one option out of my pain. I was responsible for all that had gone wrong in my life. The pain was too much to bear. I had never completed anything; I was a liar, a criminal, I underachieved all my life, I was the black sheep of my family, my choices, my life, my careers, all came down to my final choice: suicide.

I drank a bottle of Stolichnaya vodka, it was just short of a liter, and I had just under three bottles of Vicodin (just shy of 90 or so), about 30 or so Ultram and a few other pills that I had been prescribed for my back pain. I changed into some swim trunks, ran a nice hot bath, made three goodbye calls, locked the deadbolt to my front door, secured my three windows, and promptly laid in the tub and waited to die. The water expanded every vein in my body to more efficiently funnel the poison. For a life that spiraled out of control, I finally took control and wanted out. I just remember getting sleepy and fading into a slumber for what felt like a brief time; sweet relief to such a wretched life. I could hear men shouting, women crying, and sharp pounding on my chest as in my tiny one bedroom apartment, there was Austin's finest, and first responders trying to resuscitate me. I couldn't focus on much, but I did see two of my former girlfriends there, and a firefighter held me in his arms. I was rushed into an ambulance as the last thing I saw was my girlfriend who didn't stop searching for me, my parents on the other hand were still at their home, unnerved by my disappearing act. They were accustomed to me going on a self-indulgent sabbatical. I would remain at South Austin Hospital for a few days or so, in the ICU unit.

Most near death experiences start with a bright light or some kind of paranormal out of body experience where you see your body from some sort of external or lofty perspective. Maybe some people hear choirs or angels, perhaps they see their life in a fast video clip of all the people they knew, or the deeds or unfinished deeds in their lives. My fleeting movie clip was more like a David Lynch's Eraserhead. In black and white, there was no sound, just figures looking up and unable to move. As if they saw all they ever wanted in their whole lives, yet just staring longingly, with all desire, and unable to move or attain it. I was 27 years old. On March 26, I awakened to see my girlfriend and my mother at my bed side. I remember being very angry, and not wanting see anyone. My girlfriend had bought me a copy of The Histories, by Herodotus. My mother and she were so happy and relieved to see me, I on the other hand was not. I guess in my failed mind, I got suicide wrong; what a fuck up I thought I was.

To put in context of what just happened, St. Faustina wrote on February 22 1931, "In the evening, when I was in my cell, I saw the Lord Jesus clothed in a white garment. One hand (was) raised in the gesture of blessing, the other was touching the garment at the breast. From beneath the breast, and from beneath the garment, slightly drawn aside at the breast, there were emanating two large rays, one red, one pale. In silence, I kept my gaze fixed on the Lord; my soul was struck with awe, but also with great joy." Now for my non-Catholic brothers and sisters, I would just like to humbly state for the record that what St. Faustina is talking about is divine mercy. That can be easily researched and confirmed. I don't believe I need to expand or explain the similarity between what a saint saw, and what my perspective was. That is another book for another time perhaps, but I will state that I was not a practicing Catholic at the time, and quite frankly had no idea what divine mercy was or who St. Faustina was.

Oh, how I wish I could say that I saw the truth and went to church the next day, or that I saw a bush burning and the skies part with a benevolent voice of reason and forgiveness consoling me. But on the contrary, I was angry for being alive. To complicate matters, the moment that I was stable enough to walk, the Austin Police Department showed up to escort me to the Austin State Hospital in handcuffs because it is a crime to try to kill yourself like that. In front of an already traumatized mother, I was hauled away to the state hospital. In handcuffs, and placed in the back of a police car according to police procedure, in fact the exact police procedure that I had been all too accustomed to in my early 20s!

My first experience with a psychological inpatient treatment center was very eye opening to say the least. For a man that wanted nothing more than to be in the hands of love, this is a place that love isn't found in, and by the hands of love, I mean that all I probably needed was a hug. My past experience in working in the medical field made me keenly aware of good bedside manner and poor bedside manner, and I was quite aware of the importance of preventative care and the term 'quality of care.' So, I have placed myself in the most improbable and most unlikely of circumstances in the state run facility here in Austin, Texas. I understand the difference between underpaid, overworked and just people who don't have any compassion due to the unpleasantness of the mentally ill patients. I believe we are all aware of the importance that our nation places on all of the above mentioned terms. If one wants, they can research where our leaders vote on social welfare programs. In fact, my story isn't too different from most that are run through the gamut of psychological care in America. If you want compassion when you feel down, you either have great insurance coverage or you are stuck with state run facilities. The differences in the quality of care are as distinct as the great divide that separates our great country. It is not an issue of race, but rather one of class and status. The behaviors that are encouraged and learned would be debilitating and stifling for many, many years. This pattern of medication, counseling, yoga and psychiatric doctor visits is probably familiar to many Americans. My ten years plus of working in the medical field had definitely taught me the difference, and here I was experiencing it firsthand. So my truth is this: At 27, I'm given a mental health diagnosis. I have literally tried suicide twice, and probably had contemplated it more than I could count. I will skip the perils of my three years of total mental incapacitation of my mental faculties and this most isolated period of my life. I mean there is literally nothing of note to add to the plethora of articles, memoirs and studies on the effects of depression and suicide. I literally slept and tried every manner of medication made available by the medical profession.

I was desperate for some kind of solution, since my final solution didn't work. I had significant self-worth issues, my future wife left me two weeks into my stay at the state hospital back in April of 2003. She bought me a pepperoni pizza and a note that explained that she had to do what was best for her. To be totally honest, I wasn't too hurt or angry, in fact, it taught me an important lesson. And that is that it is OK for healthy people to cut the cord and leave when someone is unhealthy. I got the message loud and clear, I was the toxic one. So, I spent the next three years in a zombie like state that consisted of very little growth. My daily routine consisted of taking 1200 mg of Seroquel, 30 mg of Abilify, of Trilafon, of Lithium, 300mg of Wellbutrin, and 2mg of Risperidone, which left me an antisocial morbidly obese man of 190 pounds on a frame that stood only 5' 6" tall. The fact that I can remember this exact dosage and medicine combination should be enough to emphasize my desperation. Shocking to me is the expediency with which I typed this. I became so desperate that I tried my Catholic faith for the first time since my youth. My mom had always been faithful even in her suffering. I know at times that it was her prayers that kept me alive. She had always been a prayerful woman, attended church every Sunday, and had shown me how to pray. So, I attended a group conference in Omaha, NE, hosted at a retreat center there. I had no idea what to expect. In Austin, my mother had attended these local groups that met once a week. I had been curious, and was prayed over by many in her group. I knew my heart was calloused and closed, but damn I was desperate. Ever since I was a child, I had witnessed my mother's prayer life, meaning that I had seen many, many different forms of prayer and witnessing. My Christian brothers and sisters know what I mean. For me, listening to people speak in tongues, faint in the spirit, and pray rosaries, was not foreign to me. In fact, I was very curious and blind at the same time. I didn't want to believe that a simple solution was all that was needed for my unique and complicated circumstances. The void in my life could in no way be solved by such simpletons and archaic methods. I was so special, oh yes, that I suffered from terminal uniqueness!

I traveled with my mom to Nebraska. I attended the 'Fires of Hope' conference in 2006, at the now Quest Center in downtown Omaha. The retreatants numbered over 3,000 strong. I couldn't believe it! Mother Nadine Brown was opening the conference in her most gentle and loving way. There was a full band and screen projection with lyrics and hundreds of priests and nuns from around the world. I had never seen my faith expressed in this way. Joel Osteen's got nothing on this genuine, gentle, kind and open display of love. Believe me, I took any suggestion at this point, so I'm not ashamed to say I even gave him a chance. There was no pretense about Mother Mary, the Holy Spirit, nor Christ. It wasn't an exclusive thing that was predestined for a select few. This loving community showed me how to open my heart and love again. I was moved by the talks on the gifts of the Holy Spirit, testimonies of love and faith in the most trying circumstances. For the first time in my life, I was introduced to the gifts of the Holy Spirit, which are piety, wisdom, fortitude, knowledge, fear of the Lord, counsel and understanding. The Catholic faith was on full display and that was only the first day! Oh my! The next day was more talks, a healing mass and confessions. I had never seen my faith in action before in a way that made total sense to me. I learned how to journal, I met fantastic people from all over the world, and by the third day Mom and I returned to Austin. It was so inspiring. I was in the car heading back to my mom's home in Lockhart, TX. The town looked different, I felt different, and I acted differently. The Lord had welcomed me back into the flock with total loving, and forgiving arms. I was truly a prodigal son who was welcomed back with a giant feast, and my life was given a new direction. I was spirit filled for the first time since I was a child of five preaching the word of God to other children.

So within a week of returning from the conference, I did as instructed; I got a spiritual director. I went to my church in Lockhart, St Mary's of the Visitation. Father Robert Becker was the pastor there. I was prompt, bright eyed, and hit him with two questions that had been on my mind. Right off the bat, I asked him what the Pillar of Fire was, because when I had learned to journal, and that is what God had called me. Father Becker didn't even blink and he went straight to the book of Exodus. He then explained to me that as the Hebrews were fleeing Egypt, that there would be column of cloud that would guide them in the daytime. In the night would be a column of fire to guide them in the night. Now, I know what you're thinking: How can God call me that? Or how can I know what God thinks or calls me? If you're curious, just follow my lead and ask a priest. They won't mind. To me it was the beginning of a call to the religious life. To be a light in a time of darkness.

My second question was, "What does Agnus Dei mean?" and thus began one of the most influential and meaningful relationships I will ever know. This man of faith taught me how to be a man. Father Becker is a man who was very reverent and spiritual. Those in the central Texas area know who this man is and hold him in high regard. In this first meeting, I learned so much about prayer. I learned at least four different types, I got most of my questions answered and I started to feel some semblance of that oh so elusive peace that seemed like a mirage in the desert to me; something unattainable. Speaking metaphorically of desserts and mirages, during my faithless journey to that point, I learned to love my chaos and seemed to believe that I thrived in it. That metaphor is speaking loudly to me now, because once I started to put down the drama, I made more room for God. On one of our meetings, Father Becker took me on a hike through the state park in Lockhart, as he showed me the beauty of nature and how God was ever so present in nature. At the time, I was about 31 and he was almost double my age. I had to ask him several times to slow down, again this was the man with boundless strength in the gentlest way. He took time to share with me the meaning of meekness, solitude, nature, joy and taking care of my body. All of those things that my biological father never took the time to share with me, I mean my dad didn't even take time with me to show me how to shave! This form of love was so freeing and beautiful to me. He was tough on me, not just in hiking, but in the way I prayed and spoke the word of God. He encouraged my writing and slowed my diction. I wanted to be him so much! This busy man of God took time from his herd to show me the little things that this 'gifted' child didn't know. Like Terese of the Little Flower, he took the time to show me little things with great love, and it made the biggest difference in my life. I fully give him credit for making me the man I am today, and he remained one of my best friends to this day! Can I get an amen for brotherly love? Or in his case, fatherly love. [*]

---

[*] Father Robert Becker died on January 25 2018, at the age of 71. He was born on November 9 1946, in Dallas, Texas. He earned a bachelor's degree in 1969 from St. Edward's University in Austin, Texas, and in 1979 he earned his master's degree in Divinity at the St. Meinrad School of Theology in Indiana. He was ordained a priest of the Diocese of Austin on June 16 1979. Father Becker was one of the most influential people in my life. On a personal note, I feel like I have to mention this story. One day in 2017, Father Becker, my mother, Sister Lorena and I went to have lunch at Luby's. The first thing we did was to stand over our meal and pray in thanksgiving over our meal. It was amazing as I had never done that before. The eyes of the entire dining area were upon us. Even I was a bit self-conscious about it, but I didn't mind at all. We sat down and had a gregarious lunch filled with laughter and joy. It was not done with any pretense, it was just spontaneous. As I am an observant person, I noticed a scowl from two ladies sitting in the corner, both with multiple piercings, tattoos and very short buzz cuts. To my right was a man in a wheelchair with his wife or caretaker sitting next to him, looking in what appeared to be admiration. There was a couple of bikers also present that I could see in my periphery. As people were leaving, they would come over to our table and shake our hands and commented on our joyful nature and what a pleasure it was to witness. The man in the wheelchair also came by with gratitude.

As I recover from the tears I have just shed over remembering my spiritual father, I had made a conscious decision to follow the Lord and expand on my knowledge of the Holy Spirit. I had been so blind, so misled, so obtuse to the love and mercy of the Lord. I was on the way to experiencing a new life in Christ. And I had made the decision to become a Deacon in the Catholic Church. Then on May 2 2007, I was drinking some wine at my home in Lockhart. I had two bottles of wine and I was feeling good, free and I had a very nice time. I had taken my meds and was asleep when my next recollection was that I was behind the wheel of my car and found myself heading to Austin at

---

For some reason, a few others came by to acknowledge us all. The two women that were together didn't stop by, for unexplained circumstances, but at the same time did motion a nod out of respect from a distance. That was an amazing feeling of community for all of us there at the restaurant. What the table didn't know was the amount of suffering at our table, meaning that Father who was to my left was suffering from leukemia, my mom who was newly widowed was across from me, Lorena who was to my right had broken most of the bones in her body in a ferocious car accident some years prior and that enlightened her to become a nun, and you are reading my suffering. For whatever reason, people gravitated to our peace, joy and love for one another. I know that's exactly what the world needs now. As much as I know Father Becker, I bet he would've loved to hold a healing mass right there for anyone that wanted some prayer. So, we spent the entire day together praying laughing, crying and we all got a special blessing from him. Father showed us his garden. I tasted a fig for the first time, and that was the last time I saw him in person outside of church.

around 3am. I am forever grateful that I didn't kill anyone or go to Austin for what I knew my desire was, which was to go to the dope house. It had been a little over four years since I had inhaled that poison. I had held true to my desire to stay free of that evil chemical. That following Tuesday, I checked myself into an outpatient program and followed the all-too-familiar path that I had tried since 2003, which was psychology and medicine, and of course, the 12 step meeting.

It was here, at that outpatient program, that I would meet my future first wife. It was what was deemed a dual diagnosis program of mental illness and addiction. I remember the first time I saw her, and we connected. She asked me one day if I could lend her a pen, and I held on to it just long enough to warmly caress her hand. We would talk every day after group and in spectacular fashion (or lack of sense, cause in the words of the immortal King of Rock N' Roll, "only fools rush in.") By November, we were married by the Justice of the Peace in Austin, Texas. Although in the preceding October, we had met with Father Becker as she was considering converting from Southern Baptist to Catholicism. And the meeting lasted roughly about 45 minutes when Father, in his most loving act of tough love, asked us to leave and promptly asked to leave. Some weeks after that encounter, I went to San Jose Church for a brief confession and it turned out that living in sin is a huge thing, and not up for discussion or interpretation, as that priest came out from behind the partition as he literally scolded me about the perils of living in sin. He then proceeded to chase me out of the confessional. I scoffed and walked away, and I didn't go back to my faith until 2016.

I am a man of few regrets, but this is one, but if I had listened to Father Becker or that priest at San Jose, I wouldn't have three beautiful children who are my most special treasures from God. Therein lies the regret I could have leveled at myself to this day, if only I had listened I'd be a better man for not suffering the slings and arrows of a six year marriage that ended in divorce. For six years we went to meetings, spent those six years trying to settle on a faith, and making babies. For six years I did the 'right' thing. I was clean, I entered Texas State as a freshman in 2013, and I was a wonderful father to four step children as well as my biological children. My ex-wife hated Lockhart, I wasn't good in bed and she quit working and got on disability, and after six years had started to cheat on me. Three months later, I relapsed on chemicals and we separated on November 13 2013. Six years of marriage, encapsulated in a few sentences for a purpose. It wasn't genuine or true love at all. It was a whirlwind of lust, struggle for control and mistrust.

It must be astonishing to some that I can only devote a few sentences to six years of marriage, but what is more important to this journey is the fact that things got darker for me in the following three years or so of my separation to final divorce and what ensues next in my life. I am very bitter about the way things are to this day. The most blatant misuse of free will was yet to come, and I had no idea what this road of humility would lead to. The brief taste of spiritual awakening kept me thirsting for more love. The dissolution of my marriage after six years would be hard on me. I felt responsible, and here I was again using and abusing chemicals and my body. I was angry for being alive, angry at God and the church's stupid rules for marrying outside the faith, and here I was a weekend dad again. The fact that I felt so alienated for thinking that my faith was strong, and that I had some sort of entitlement for suffering as much as I did, and I felt I was due some sort of reprieve for all my good deeds. I found myself delving into darker and darker shades of sex and drugs.

I can only speak for my actions, not that of my ex-wife's, but I can observe to this day that the reception I received from her was not one of mercy or love when I explained to her that after six years of living a clean and sober lifestyle, that I had relapsed. Three months prior to my relapse, I had discovered that my ex-wife was cheating on me. Truth is, we didn't share the same faith, and truth is we didn't get along, truth is she never loved me. Truth is, I know in all honesty she never loved me, because it explains her behavior toward me and why she married me so quickly. I know because I read her diary that she left in my house when she packed up both flat screens, all of the Blu-Ray, DVDs and anything of value, as she walked out the door.

So, we separated on November 13, 2013, and that day started as any other day would. My ex-wife took the children up to San Angelo, TX, to visit her family. And I was alone, three months of trying to bring trust back into our marriage, and my life starts to take a turn for a really bizarre turn. Now I fully believe that once trust is gone, it never comes back. It is a little bit like respect. If it is gone it rarely, if ever, comes back. For me, this is the turning point, the proverbial worm turning, the hitting lows just to rise up (yet again). This is a total mind meld of the 'highest' order, I crack me up.

After six years of doing the right thing, of going to recovery meetings, being a good family man and a faithful husband, I relapsed and went for a four day binge. I guess anyone would do what I did, I feel that I'm just honest about it in a world where sex, drugs and vices are driven into our psyches on a daily basis, and I did what a lot of people do. Hear me out, please. I went to solicit a working woman, and as it turned out she was actually very attractive. Let me preface this with the institution of rules that I had for myself. This is a practice that has stuck with me to this day. I had two rules on my excursion, and they were no alcohol or cocaine, so the rest was on the menu. Needless to say, it leaves a cornucopia of chemicals, but to my credit I held fast to those two rules. So, when I met this woman, she offered me crystal meth, and that was my next vice that would engulf the next two years or so.

For a man with four different personality traits the introduction of amphetamines exacerbated and amplified my extroverted side. The one that was the life of the party, the one that gets things going and made it fun for everyone else found limitless opportunity in this drug. So maybe after a six year bit of clean time, crystal meth was the wrong thing, but that being said, instead of my sex filled drug thing that I always did, this four day binge wasn't about sex. In fact, I didn't have any sex. In fact, I spent most of that time naked in front of a mirror overpaying for drugs and learning how to use my new chemical of choice. My true number one relationship at that point was one with chemicals. I had a void that I was unable to fill all my life. I had a pain in my heart that I was unable to articulate with anyone. I had no idea what drove this immense sadness, as I repeated the sins of my past and took them to new lows. Another one of my rules was that I wasn't going to kill myself. And yet, for the pain I endured in my marriage, I found a new level of self-respect and a chilling way of dealing with people after I learned the greatest gift from my ex-wife, after my three beautiful children, was manipulation. I guess I'm thankful, but truth be told, it taught me how to recognize it in the most subtle way. And I applied it to my newfound respect for myself. And I became something almost extraordinary. I had always been a little streetwise, now I was bold in ways unimaginable to me prior to my marriage. I had always been deemed 'gifted,' and now I was almost drunk with my newfound glory. Couple that with a chemical that basically woke me up. So, thus begins my love hate relationship with this drug. The rush of serotonin and the primal ecstasy of sex was exactly what the doctor ordered for me, actually what I ordered for myself. On an all too frequent and regular basis. What I deemed my two to three days of debauchery, sandwiched in between visits with my children because my soon-to-be ex-wife couldn't wait to get out of the picture or rather get me out of the picture. For me, the pain of a failed marriage was too much to bear, and I was taking all the steps to ensure that no woman would ever hurt me again. And that also still holds true for me to this day.

According to Isaac Newton, an object in motion tends to stay in motion, but even the laws of physics have to be suspended for a man whose passions had completely consumed him. I was abruptly awakened from this slumber on March 5 2015. Now, up to this point I was just having fun, sleeping with women and turning people on to my new bravery and lust for life. I'm living my life like a rap song, minus the endowment and the jewelry. But this day is probably the hardest day I have ever known in my life.

I have heard and read about sinking feelings and surreal moments that forever alter the course of one's life. For me, it was my youngest daughter coming up to me and saying the words, "Dada, I hurt down there." Those are the most bone chilling, bloodcurdling words I've ever heard in my life. Now, I kept telling her to go change out of those jeans that she was wearing, but she kept pointing down to her crotch and wouldn't stop saying that phrase. I was with my mother at her home in Lockhart and we both had this confused look on our faces. My beautiful daughter is four years old at the time. And what ensues is a trip to Dell Children's Hospital in Austin, Texas. All I will say about that is that no four-year-old should have a fluid exam. At this point, I won't go into what pain it is to hear that from an innocent child. Now those words alone haunt me to this day, and as I can only speak for myself, that is what I will stay on point about. Truth is, it is too hard to write about at this time. I moved to Dallas some days after this point. I have heard some parents say at this point that they would rather their child had died than to go through the pain of something like that. I'm not entirely sure that I agree with that, but truth be told, my own personal trauma was just unfolding.

Some months later in June 2015, I had a mental breakdown. It was the end of an emotional night with my best friend at the time that ended in some sort of breakdown, where at this point all I knew was pain and deep, deep, deep sorrow. All I could see was pain in my life. No one could help me find a way out of it. So, I did what I had become accustomed to doing, I checked into an institution to get medical help for problems that I had no way of grasping. I managed to drive my car into south Dallas, into a hospital called Timberlawn. I ended up staying inpatient for 21 days. Now, I go in for my usual diagnosed symptoms of some mental disorder or something, some counseling, medications and the usual array of modern treatments for symptoms that ail a majority of Americans. I'm God's perfect idiot because Timberlawn is one of the best trauma centers in the country. I was officially diagnosed with DID, PTSD and major clinical depression. DID is dissociative identity disorder which is brought upon by sexual trauma. I was sexually abused as a child by my father between the ages of 8 to 12. Finally, years of therapy, group meetings, prayer groups, inpatient stays, the gamut of the best pharmaceuticals both prescribed and otherwise, suicide attempts and one near death experience came down to one cold hard truth, and that was that it wasn't my fault. Came to recall that is why there is such a blank period in my life. That is why I was so filled with pain, and I could never find joy in any of this life. This is the truth of why my dad and I never got along, and all I could do was run. Not only from him, but from everything I ever started, from boy scouts to relationships.

As I mentioned at the onset of my story, my father died this year on February 18, 2017, in Austin, Texas. What happened to me over the past couple of years is unreal and unbelievable to the point that love and mercy couldn't possibly be the solutions to these very serious situations and trauma. I am, by no means, suggesting a blind faith kind of way; that all you need is prayer and good intentions such that a meme might do. I do give all credit to God for all He has done in my life, for which there is no doubt, that the hand of God has touched my life. That being so boldly stated, what is the solution for me could very well be the solution for a great many men and women who suffer more or less of similar traumas or violations of body. I am going to take some steps backward in the story to illustrate some of the more spiritual gifts that came into my life thanks to little acts of love shown to me by nuns and priests who took the time to pray with me.

Follow me back to the fall of 2013, and I have just relapsed for the first time in six years. I'm naked in front of a mirror learning this new chemical with a very beautiful Latina in the bed inviting me to come and share it with her. This wasn't our last encounter, but we never had sex since; instead, we began a friendship that turned into a sort of business relationship, as through friends of hers I learned the essence of what working women do. I began many relationships (some sexual, most not), wherein, I learned the trade. Around the same time, my best friend, unbeknownst to me, was also getting into the lifestyle as well. For many years, we became close friends and mutual business partners. What started out as a hustle turned into a very beneficial relationship of sex and drugs that benefited us and anyone we came in contact with. I mean, I broke bread with the best of them. Hotel parties, meeting tons of people, sometimes just giving drugs away. I learned two things during those years following my divorce, and that was two professions of drug dealing and pimping. This 'gifted' child of God was doing some very demeaning things with the 'best' of intentions and most misguided charity. I will NOT glorify or go into details as to how a man of my stature and laidback attitudes got himself into this lifestyle, but I was engulfed in it.

I loved the thrill of it all, and I was taking out my resentments on what I felt were weak men and have the maximum access of all the vices life could offer in cities from San Antonio to Houston, to Dallas. I had a network of friends I could rely on at most turns to get me high, and I would help them out as well. I bet it sounds pretentious or naively to say that we helped each other out or that I found people to love in such a world as that of drugs and prostitution, but there were some good people wrapped up in that lifestyle. For those of us that had been hurt, and had shared so much pain, I would say that was the tie that bound some of our friendships and business relations. Many of us bore the same scars from the fallout of emotional pain and suffering. For example, I met a few associates who were former military that had served in the two gulf wars, in fact one was a former medic, who taught me how to better inject myself. Many of the women that I had met had been abused or sexually assaulted, like me. One man whom I spent Christmas eve with had a daughter who was sexually assaulted, so in a sense I hope all involved were mutually satisfied, and I pray these days for them and their loved ones. To be honest, I miss and loved their company. As for the thrill of it all, I must reiterate that this isn't a glorification of the lifestyle, but an absolute truth. I recall NWA and more current hip hop stars such as The Weeknd, or Kendrick Lamar, when they sing of the survival or even conquest over the prevailing evil that is on the streets. Their music is for me, totally understandable. I was granted a very brief insight into life of the music that was written about the very real struggle for love, money, and addiction. Those emotions and situations are very real. Now for the spiritual axioms that are related to my particular journey of faith.

The main point to share is that it was one of love, that love was a part of most of what I did. And I fully believe, that the tiniest of seeds that were planted by Father Becker and others of my faith with the greatest of love, were definitely coming to fruition even as the world would most condemn my lifestyle choices, as I do, because it is a dangerous, idiotic and cold-blooded business. As many wonderful people that I met, I know I met some major assholes and downright evil people. At some points in San Antonio, I would give out copies of Mother Nadine's books to people I would meet. As for hooking up in the digital age, was an online Don Juan, if a woman and I wouldn't have sex we would talk and have a good time anyway. I would end up with some genuine friendships for sure.

By the time 2015 rolled around, I was starting to have images of my father behind me; the smell of his breath, the feel of his face and of course, images of his anatomy. To be honest, I thought it was the drugs. On April 23 2015, the day before my 40th birthday, my father and I had a confrontation in the house in Lockhart, Texas. All I could feel was immense hatred for the man, for at this point I couldn't get the images of his body and feel out of my head. I remember shouting to him that I hated him. I went after him, and my sister and nephew, who was fifteen at the time, jumped on me and all three were punching, kicking me and hurting me. My mother witnessed all of this, and I know that it was too much for her. I left Lockhart with broken ribs and a bloody nose. The damage is still felt to this day, and we have not been a family since, fact is we never really were one. My mom rented a rental car for me and I drove back to Dallas with physical pain and anxiety that brought upon IBS for the first time in my life; it struck me in that rental car that night as drove back to Dallas. The cold hard truth to be revealed in Dallas just two months later, that I was a victim of sexual abuse. I spent that summer and fall of 2015 just trying to get out of my head. In each random online hookup, or chance meeting that I pursued, turned into a search for the basics of a relationship; I didn't care about the sex as much as I just needed a damn hug. As it turns out, drugs and sex are much easier to find.

I spent those remaining months of my lease in Dallas just trying to get out of my head. I think I initially had that old recovery refrain of service as a recurring mantra, and the total understanding that I knew how far I could fall if I let my depression get the best of me. It sure doesn't make sense, but I feel I did some good out there in the process. I would let people stay at my place for weeks on end. There was the activity of drugs and sex around me. But really, the more I got to know the people I tried to help and love; I learned about myself and my boundaries. It definitely takes character to do the hazardous things I did, while maintaining some level of discipline of not letting the drugs get the better of me. I learned to apply rules to my drug use, and casual sex, and online dating thing that I was doing on a daily basis. I was like Jason Statham in 'The Transporter,' driving anyone from gang members, drugs, to escorts all over Texas. I got paid in drugs, money and sometimes sex. The lifestyle was a rush when I avoided the authorities or impending danger. I rewarded my righteous activities with one hell of an IV methamphetamine addiction. I looked like hell and weighed about 121 pounds. I think in the year 2015, I didn't sleep but maybe a third of the year. My initial search for that proverbial heart of gold in the underbelly of Dallas, Texas, meeting and subsequently falling in love with a porn star, doing more and more drugs, but still not drinking or smoking pot. I didn't want anything to slow me down, or at least that is what I told myself.

I had two turning points in my extended leave of sanity in Dallas, which some would say could be moments of clarity. On Christmas eve of 2015, I spent that evening with two people that I had a working relationship with. We got high and exchanged stories of suffering. It was like a group therapy session, but we weren't afraid of triggering people. We had the PTSD, trauma, victim of assaults, issues that most closed-hearted people would say doesn't merit the attention of our government. The war stories and the shedding of tears did bring us closer together, but I know that was just a moment that was shared by three people in a constant whirlwind of drama, that has life or death consequences when drugs and money are concerned, but it was one of the moments where I realized that being vulnerable had its merits. It was the beginning of my deconstruction, and little did I know, my rebirth. I call it an epiphany, but not in the religious sense. For me, it was a moment of self-realization that I was more than what I had been exhibiting in this life. I feel like it was the first time in a very long time that I felt God speaking to my heart. I called my mother some days later and professed my newfound direction. I'm sure she was so exhausted from my constant struggle for righteous living, but I knew something was different. My slow paced crawl back to my faith consisted of visits to Father Luca Simbula, that preceding Easter. I found him out of sheer desperation. On Easter Sunday, I was conflicted about my daughter's outcry that previous month, and I was so frustrated with looking for support for parents and children who are victims of sexual abuse. So, that evening, I called Catholic churches around me, and St Rita's church was the closest to my apartment. I called the bereavement option for deaths and funeral arrangements and by a miracle, I got in touch with Father Luca. He didn't judge me or scold me for not following protocol, instead he invited me over to his office that very next day, thus beginning another relationship with a very spiritual man of God who could read me like a book. I would go seek him out for direction, much like I had in Father Becker. He taught me so much! Regardless of the condition I was in, I would confess to Father Luca what I had been doing. He's a Jesuit Priest, he does great work these days at St. Augustine Catholic Church in Dallas these days, so I know that he was aware of the frail bag of bones that I was so desperately trying to hide with my hoodie and baggy cargo shorts in the middle of summer. I wore long sleeves to cover my track marks on my arms. Father Luca would give me the sage and loving wisdom that I am accustomed to receiving from such wonderful men who devote their lives to God. Here was another man who took time out of being an associate pastor at St. Rita's Catholic Church, which was just under two miles from my apartment in North Dallas.

The second turning point in my journey was a situation in January of 2015, wherein, I was beginning to branch out into fencing stolen goods. I had met a wonderful couple at a corner store one night that was right down the street from my apartment. I don't find these things as mere coincidence, as I believe that there are no coincidences in God's world. As fate, coincidence, or divine providence would have it, these young ladies did the same chemicals I did. I'm not exactly sure what draws people to a convenience store at 4 a.m., but I'm sure that is more to do with common interests rather than coincidence or divine providence. All kidding aside, here is the spiritual truth for me at this point. I am not living with any moral compass, I'm like one of those pawn shop show guys without the TV show. This 'gifted' child of God, is now selling electronics and moving stolen goods, selling drugs, letting prostitutes work in his apartment, running an illegal taxi service, while trying to kill an unfathomable abyss of loneliness and pain. I don't think there is a drug or sex act that could give any comfort.

So my newfound 'friends' came up to my apartment at some point later in the week with a joyous bounty of stolen merchandise. There was apparel, electronics and a purse. In the excitement of this huge 'score' when the purse spilled over during the apparent glee of one of the women finding shoes that fit her, out fell this person's money, identification, and most importantly, prayer cards and rosary. I stood there flabbergasted, and for some unknown reason to me, disgusted. Now, out of all of the heinous shit I did back then, was this 'score' the worst I had seen? No, absolutely not, but the prayer cards that fell out of this were a Saint Michael the archangel, a Pope Francis, and unbeknownst to me, a Saint Benedict card. Now, the first two, I knew well, the latter, I did not know. To top it off, the last card was in Spanish, which I still have difficulty reading. After a closer look at the contents of the purse, I could deduce that this person was of Guatemalan descent, or perhaps even an illegal immigrant. I could tell by the loose Guatemalan currency that was separated from a torn envelope. The coldest part of the prayer cards that hit me hardest, was that it humanized the 'score' and made this person human in my eyes. I could imagine this person's horror at all that was missing of their possessions. Maybe this woman's last international calling card before payday was now being used for another purpose by the perpetrators of this crime. Perhaps, there was a family that would worry for quite some time until they heard from their relative in from the United States. I immediately asked newfound friends to leave and take their 'score' with them. I kept the prayer cards. I still have them with me today as reminder not to discount anyone's humanity.

My mother on the other hand, knew that I was not doing well. She would call only when my father wasn't around; because after our last confrontation, he wanted nothing to do with me. That made no difference to me, as he was absent for most of my life anyway. I didn't see my dad or speak to him until almost a full year later, which was full of self-discovery and spiritual growth. I finally was able to leave the lifestyle behind on February 8 2016, which coincided with my lease being up in my North Dallas apartment.

I'm so glad I left Dallas, because everything was way too easy there. If it was easy for a nobody like me, could you imagine what it's like to be a Dallas Cowboy football player; meaning, no wonder they get into so much trouble. Shit, I'm not famous nor do I have the body of a model, and it was very easy for me to have fun. Couple that with the fact that I was slowly realizing that all of my sadness wasn't my fault, and that the party was just getting was fun and seemingly without end. Thanks be to God for my lease ending. If I didn't leave Dallas when I did, I surely would've been dead. That is my truth for sure, and no one can convince me otherwise.

So, thus begins a new leg of my journey, one that moves from a physically pleasing one to a more spiritual basis, which was basically the one thing I had never enthusiastically embraced or followed through on. When I left Dallas, I knew I needed help with my conditions, and I made the command decision that I would go to any length to find a solution to my PTSD and depression. I also knew that I had to completely stop the chemicals. Armed with my newfound discovery of my emptiness and sadness, along with my new confidence and healthy respect for myself, I knew I couldn't place myself into that victimhood as I had so witnessed many others in my life. I do give much of that credit to my years in recovery group, but that being said, I never subscribed to that blanket disease concept that that wonderful program places on everyone that walks in the door. I don't believe I've ever had the severe withdrawal symptoms that so many of my brothers and sisters had. I have seen them firsthand, so I know that recovery group couldn't fully fill the void in my life. Counseling and yoga only went so far, and I have had some wonderful yoga experiences, but my faith, as far as I practiced it, had never been put into motion.

I leave Dallas in an exhausted and vacant state of mind. I left all I had behind; I packed my 2015 Toyota Camry with a firm intention of leaving all of that behind me in both a literal and figurative sense, and I drove to Galveston to literally wash Dallas off of me. I laid down in the Gulf of Mexico and gave myself a literal cleansing. I actually ended up driving around Texas for the next six weeks. From sleeping on couches, to parking lots across Texas, something was happening to me; the desire for sex was leaving me. I know that my scarred psyche was preventing me from enjoying the basic pleasures of sex. I was losing that desire mainly because I couldn't get the images of my father out of my head. So, I went in search of answers. First thing I did was check into detox in Austin, Texas. I also got as many labs done as possible, with my bad back and physical ailments and all. I wanted to do a cartwheel when I got my HIV blood work back, and it was negative. I made a conscious choice to refrain from sex for a while, little did I know that it would mean for me no sex until marriage, but I am saving myself for marriage, truth be told. And I started taking care of my diabetes, and actually eating healthier. My circle of friends started to change, which basically meant I was alone, but something was different. All of those little things that people of faith showed me, I applied in Dallas; meaning, I tried to help out as many people as I could that crossed my path. What happened, I believe, was that I applied Catholic principles along with a hybrid of service engrained in me through years of service in recovery programs. The main focus for me in Dallas and beyond has always been to get out of my head. For a dreamer like me, that is deadly. And the moment I start to think I'm God, I'm screwed, at least that is what I fully believe now. See, my prayer about five years ago was this, "God, show me humility." As I know now, I don't ask for that anymore at all. It is now this, and just this, "You know my heart, God." And I immediately pray for others. I guess that is how I learned to pray, out of necessity, and the methods of getting out of self-centered behavior.

After my solo road trip across Texas that ended in an extended stay at a detox center in Austin, Texas, I visited my mother in San Antonio. As I have previously mentioned, my mother and I had very limited communication because my father and I weren't speaking, so we had to meet covertly at my aunt's home in North San Antonio. It was so good to see her with clear eyes. We hugged, we shared tears, and vented to each other about our state of affairs. In layman's terms, that means discussing my father; something that we have always done together. I was emphatically expressing to my mom how I had changed for good, and that I knew I was on a new road. That is the rub for someone who had always said that, and yet had really not had much progress to show for it. It is like that boy crying wolf ten thousand times too many. It must have been a total challenge for my mom to accept this change in me. To her loving credit, she never gave up on me. So we were sitting on my aunt's sofa, and I pulled out that prayer card that I had held onto since I found it in Dallas. I pulled out the one of St. Benedict in which the prayer was written in Spanish, so I asked her for a translation. I also asked her to tell me the story of St. Benedict.

My mom proceeded to educate me on the life of this saint, who is considered one of the greatest minds in our faith. My mom told me the story of this monk of noble descent that went to live in a cave for three years, because he was dissatisfied with life in Rome. She continued to tell me St. Benedict's story, and it was fascinating to me. I wanted to lay on her lap like a child at bedtime, but my mom and I aren't very affectionate. She went on to say how the people of the surrounding community wanted him to lead an abbey in the nearby town. The great saint knew that the disposition of those monks at that abbey weren't at all like his, and he was very reluctant. Saint Benedict was moved at the communities' desire to have him lead it, so the great saint succumbed. Now to me, what makes the lives of saints so appealing are those improbable circumstances that surround them, and what separates them from us is their bravery to go with their faith. That is what is so misconstrued by many who think we worship saints. Oh my, how do things get so twisted? Anyway, I sat there enthralled by my mother's recount of how the monks at that abbey tried to poison Benedict, and as he prayed over the glass of wine, it shattered! I was hooked from that moment on. My curiosity for this saint has become a healthy obsession with me, and truth be told, this obsession is much better than my prior endeavors. To this day, I read as much as I can on him, and I wear his medals around my neck. What fascinates me about my change of perspective was that it was the first time that my heart was open to listening to a story like that. It was a story that I could relate to, because since August of 2015, my eyes had begun opening up to a new life; one that was slowly lifting a fog of blindness and narrow scope of the way life actually is. I was blinded by money, sex, drugs, codependency, depression, physical pain and abuse. My struggle for control in all of these things led me to one truth: let it go!

So naturally, I end up traveling back to Omaha, Nebraska, where I had attended that conference of spirituality that had changed my life so much back in 2006. At this point, I had traveled as far west as Salt Lake City, Utah and up to Marquette, Michigan, searching for healing and answers. By this time, it was mid May 2016, and I drove down from Michigan all the way down to Omaha, Nebraska. I had placed over 46,000 miles or so on my 2015 Camry in one year! I saw a great deal of this country and met many wonderful people whom have left a lasting impression on me. I decided to go on a week-long silent retreat with the beautiful souls that added so much to my life at that very special recovery center. The remaining members still host retreats there and spiritual workshops. I arrived at Bellwether on May 9 2016, just the following Monday evening before Pentecost which was on May 17 2016. And in the days in between, I was only allowed to speak with my spiritual advisor for one hour per day, the rest was silence for me.

With the help of my spiritual advisor, I worked on my fears and spirit. My journey felt like it was just beginning. Now I know, people have spiritual awakenings, and things are never the same after that. As I am learning, and now fully believe, with the Holy Spirit, anything is possible. I believe that we all have experiences in the spiritual realm, but that we often neglect them or don't want to believe them, or as I see with my new heart and eyes, we are overstimulated, oversexed, and just downright blinded by lies and deception. There are good things in this life that don't require six easy payments plus shipping and handling, nor do I need any further validation in my life from friends, family, or even a girlfriend, because I know who has me all the days of my life! There is a margin of time that I believe when something deep and effectual occurs in one's life, and we as children of God have to capitalize on that moment to participate in our salvation; meaning strike while the iron is hot (to borrow from our modern vernacular). That is why we are so on fire when things like this happen to us, but for me the true test of being a true disciple is when the rubber meets the road and shit hits the fan. God gives us that fuel to encounter anything that comes for us, and that by our true faith we are saved and on a journey that is never ever boring, because that is life with the Lord. That for me, is true providence!

May 17, 2016 started out as any Pentecost Sunday I guess, for my non-Christian brothers and sisters this is the birth of our church, where the Holy Spirit descends on the apostles while in the upper room. For me, I was on the second to last day of my silent retreat, and it was going well considering it was a miracle in and of itself that a man like me could keep this much silence, but it was deepening my faith for sure! As per usual, the hermits in Omaha would drive me and the only other male retreat attendee in a small compact car which the young man and I were in the back seat of. It was a wonderful mass at Our Lady of Lourdes, near Creighton University. In fact, it was a very beautiful mass, in fact, I don't believe I have ever been to a bad one, maybe an off-key sermon, but NEVER a bad mass. Two hermits and I, and a young man were heading back to Bellwether, and we were passing Creighton University. I looked up at it in my silence and had a boy's recall of wanting to attend that university as a child. I looked up to the sky, as I had marveled at all of the beauty in the sky. I immediately drifted into a very beautiful calm and very peaceful rest. I had an appointment with my spiritual director to go into the chapel the night before my retreat was drawing to an end, but for me, it wasn't over by any means.

She wanted to pray for healing for me over my DID (dissociative identity disorder). What this diagnosis meant according to the wonderful treatment team at Timberlawn was that I had four distinct personalities that would manifest in me. After one hour of hypnosis at Timberlawn, I knew that I didn't want to spend my life trying to connect my distinct personas. I spent that hour back in June of 2015 crying like a child for an hour. My distinct personalities were what I deemed 'the protector,' 'the introvert,' 'the extrovert' and 'the child.' After that uneventful hour, I again made a conscious choice (free will) to give myself to God and the Holy Spirit. So, here it was almost a year later, and getting prayed upon for thousandth time in my life, my advisor prayed over me and I slumped in the front pew.

What I saw is this, and no one can convince me otherwise, and this is something that I have only spoken with priests, my mother and only two very close friends. I was slain in the spirit, to my non-Christian brothers and sisters, I fainted. For my Christian brothers and sisters, I was slain in the spirit. Now, to me it is a case of apple and oranges, because remember, I didn't believe in much other than God and love, so the rest all becomes a moot point. What happens next filled me with so much conviction that nothing will ever shake my faith! Absolutely nothing has as of yet, and my ride over the next few years is perfect example of my faith in action. And believe me it has been tested!

As I laid slain in the spirit for a second time in the day, I had what some may call a vision or images, again, it's semantics to me, I don't care what you call it but it was real. As I laid slumped on the pew, it felt to me as if new life was being breathed into me, as if Abba, the creator of all life, was giving me CPR. It felt as if my chest was rising, as if I was being administered CPR. The next thing I felt was these hands lifting me up from behind as if I was being helped up. I felt the mantle of Mother Mary over me. Thirdly, I felt huge warm, strong hands over my neck and head. My eyes, which had been shut the entire time in which all I saw was black, suddenly felt like pressure had been relieved from them and it wasn't black anymore. I felt the same hand on my heart, then the gentle hands that were holding me up, gently raised my neck to see the Eucharist and on it was the word UNITE. As clear as day, and for just a brief moment, that may have lasted about three seconds or so, I saw the face of Jesus Christ, in a way that I had never seen before in paintings, artwork, crosses,] or pictures of any kind. All I can say, is that it was so beautiful and gentle. The most accepting face of love that I can't even begin to articulate. To me, these days any statue I see of Jesus, or Mary gazing upon Him during any nativity scene makes total sense to me. I imagine that kind of like that total unfathomable gaze at beauty and love that just changes your life forever.

Now, when I actually opened my eyes, I saw my advisor in tears, and I was a changed man full of conviction of what I saw and experienced. I left Omaha the next day with a changed perception and a new life. How can one say that a life so sinful, and a life in where I did so much to please myself and no one else, that I had been changed for good? I can't even say that because my life isn't over yet, and really who is anyone to judge me or you? But we do it anyway, we judge or pass judgment on everything from politics to food, to others. We all do it, whether we care to admit it or not. And we all know that change is never easy or else everyone would do it. Lord knows I had been trying for 40 years at that point!

The first person that I saw after my experience was mother, and it didn't go as smoothly as I had intended. We got into a hellish disagreement about past wounds and things that we have never talked about. It was the first time we discussed my abuse and why I hated my father, why my nightmares occurred and why I could never sleep. My mother had a really difficult time coming to terms with all that occurred during our lives, and the only time we got to spend in 2016 was a brief road trip from Michigan to Texas. During that time on the road, I had expressed the desire to share my newfound perspective on life with my father. I also felt a strong desire to see him, hug him and express my forgiveness to him. In spite of all that had occurred in my life, it became more important for me to ask his forgiveness for my anger toward him. It was a very humbling moment for me to do that. Perhaps it was that 'on fire' moment from my spiritual experience, or whatever you want to call it. I knew that I didn't want to think too much about it, and that I wanted to do it fast like ripping off a band aid, then leaving Lockhart for good and head back to Michigan to live and heal. I was forgiving him for me and me alone; I was sick and tired of the way I had lived my life for 40 years and I was ready for it to change. During my time at the retreat, I had learned to journal with God and I had shared it with my spiritual advisor, and I knew I was journaling properly; I have come into the habit of journaling and sharing with trusted advisors.

So here is the initial plan, I was to just drive down there, drop my mom off and then leave. It is now memorial weekend in 2016. Now, let me elaborate on my belief in participating in my own personal salvation, and what I mean by being a faithful servant. I have always believed in God, even when I was at my most abusive of my free will. The seeds that my mother planted in me were deep and strong. I give her a lot of credit for standing by me when no one else did, as only a mother can. I had a soul only a mother could love. So, somewhere around the Dallas area on Interstate 35, or even earlier, my mom was in contact with my sister and father to let them know that after one year or so, since I had last seen them all, that I was on the way to see them. It was an icy reception because of that last assault before my 40th birthday, and none of us had spoken about it. I know that my dad didn't want to talk with me, and truth be told I didn't want much to see him; I mean really, who would want to see their abuser? For some reason, I was moved by the Lord, and I had an unexplainable urgency to forgive and be forgiven for my shit. I had this unbearable desire to not carry this hate anymore! I knew from my decades of therapy that if I didn't unload this, that I would surely sink and most likely die this time! I was given an opportunity to maybe not make things right, but this plan was screwed from the beginning; as I pulled into Lockhart with my mom in the passenger seat, my father was at a bar getting plastered.

Who knows what was in his head or heart, but he most definitely wasn't ready to see me. So I'm good at reading the tea leaves, and I figured that now wasn't the time so I dropped off my mother and her luggage. We did it fast because I was piping mad. Thus far in 2016, my mother and I couldn't speak freely on the phone or even in Michigan because my dad forbade it. Even though, I was the one left with broken ribs!

So here I was, ready to head back to Michigan to begin to heal, and I get a text from my mother that she had left a bag in the trunk of my car. I was about 30 miles away in a town called Kyle, TX, and I was actually driving by my children's home to see them, but no one was home so that worked out nicely. I made a safe turn around, and it actually gave me time to cool down. So I figured it was OK to go back, but my mother wanted me to hurry because my dad might be back at any moment, so of course, I was going to be brief. In the less than 45 seconds it took to grab the bag from my trunk to bring it to my mother, along my sister drives into the drive, and this awkwardness ensues since we hadn't seen each other since the broken ribs incident the day before my 40th birthday and my actual last words to my sister weren't very kind. I am a changed man with conviction galore and forgiveness on the brain, so I went to speak with her in private. I initially wanted to show her the pictures that I had taken in the year that we had been apart, but somehow, we ended up discussing Dad and the reason that I was there. I have since learned how to guard my heart and intentions, and what ensues is one more level of humility that has taken me years to attain. Being a man of few regrets, this is one of them, and I told my sister that I had felt that my father had sexually abused me, and what I thought would be a certain sense of understanding or at least a compassionate heart turned out to be a big cluster bomb, rather more like another atomic bomb; Nagasaki if you will. One thing led to another, and it was my father's turn to come home. He was stumbling and slurring his speech, and how happy he was to see me. I had the words in my heart that I had been rehearsing for two thousand miles.

I gave him a hug and whispered in his ear, "We're men, we don't have to talk about the past. If I have done anything in my life to upset or hurt you, I ask for your forgiveness." That may not make sense to many people reading this (Or one…haha!), but the truth is, he had tears of joy and hugged me and had this huge look of relief on his face that was priceless, and if there is one thing that as I write this, in my own personal search for relief and love, was this memory of when my dad woke up the next morning and I found him just staring and fumbling with a rosary, and on his face was a most gentle smile. He walked away from the dinner table, and what I saw was a rosary in the shape of a heart. This is the one memory or good thing I was searching for in my life that I will choose to remember about my dad for the rest of my life.

To me, forgiveness isn't about pardoning someone because I really don't have the power to render any judgement, the only power I have is given to me by God, and I choose Him every time to enter my heart and guide me and I lay down my life for Him and Him alone because that is the only thing that could fill the emptiness in my life. God's love and mercy, that right or wrong, I put into practice out of total desperation, for I had tried everything else that this world has to offer. I was on the road to my personal emancipation from the yoke of this life. This fairytale is far from over, and this dream of a united family fell apart that night. For whatever reason, my dad went out and got drunk (again), this had now been the third night I had stayed there when I had only wanted to stay for a couple of minutes. I was so crushed to know the all-too-familiar pattern of my father's visits to the bars. He went when he was sad, happy or bored. This habit of his always drove me crazy. I understand how it goes, I mean I really didn't need a reason to indulge and please myself. I understand my father in this way, because I freed my heart of hate. When I say that, this emotion doesn't just go away. I'm 42 years old now, and I am dealing with the various forms of anger that I allowed to permeate my thoughts and actions. It is a constant battle that I fight every morning; when I get out of bed, to people I meet on the street. It is a constant fight in my soul, but if I didn't practice what the Lord teaches, I wouldn't have made the progress I have made and continue to make on a daily basis.

For whatever reasons, my sister and I have rarely been close, and these days we don't even talk. My car wouldn't start, and I couldn't leave Lockhart as much as I wanted to. The fourth and final night in Lockhart, Texas was awful. My dad was drunk again, and I was livid and having all sorts of recall to memories long forgotten. He had gotten home at around 10 p.m., and my sister and I were on each other's nerves. She couldn't understand why I was so agitated. My sister has as bad a temper as my father and I have. I chalk that up to family tradition. We let a lifetime of frustration blow up at all the wrong times no matter how ideally we'd like to be close, it's just a fact that we are different people, and another fact of life is that oil and water don't mix. As I remember to this day, what my father's look of joy and relief as he fiddled with a rosary. I couldn't bring myself to tell my father the words of abuse and shame that he must have felt at the whole thing that must've been an acme anvil on his back as he always tried to find serenity in his life. It must hurt like hell (like the Wylie to hit the damning condemnation of shame and guilt over and over in his head that had always dragged me down as well). My sister on the other hand, felt it her duty to let him know the truth as to why I was there and took the noble cause of telling him why I was there; to address my abuse issues with him.

So, while he was very drunk no less, she shouted at the door at him as my dad and I were embraced, "He thinks you sexually abused him!" My dad released me and just wobbled as if all the life left him. The secret was out, and my dad wavered in discord as my sister then notably continued to point out how much of a liar and addict I was. For whatever moral high ground she felt she had, it destroyed all progress no matter how insignificant this may be to anyone reading this. Sexual abuse is never an easy thing to discuss or address, and there never seems to be a right time to talk about serious matters that weren't meant to be brought to light, I guess. So, I thank my sister for her beautiful, brilliant mistake because it definitely put my faith and conviction to the most stringent test.

Now the famous family temper has taken hold on us all, and my poor mother was in shock. As she has seen her dream of family taken from hopeful heights and the all-too-familiar dreadful lows. My mother did what she could and had the clarity to separate us and send me to the other house on her property for me to cool down, and for my sister and I to stop yelling and cursing at each other. So, I went to my sister's home with my tail between my legs and hurt feelings. My mission of forgiveness was an utter failure, but if I let my failures define me, I would have been dead a long time ago. That being said, I reverted to safety measures that I knew at the time, which was to call someone in recovery to help. As I hadn't been in Austin in such a long time, I really didn't have many options, but I did call an old sponsor. But not even he answered, so I was stuck there in Lockhart, TX, with nothing but my anger.

This is an excellent example of what I had truly lacked in my journey, or self-care tool kit. Restraint of my emotions has always been an issue for me. A lack of self-control in what I say and think, and who could blame me after all of the obstacles that I have had in my life. In walks with my brother-in-law, from a hard shift at work, and he was annoying me as per usual. He and I aren't particularly close either, and I picked a hell of a time to rehash family wounds with him. Now he is 5' 8", and probably weighs close to 200 pounds (I'm 5' 6", 140 pounds, so I know I wasn't that big of a threat to him). He and I got into a fight where I left with broken ribs (again), he strangled me into 'submission' (yes, he loves his MMA), and he injured me something awful. So much so, that an ambulance drove me to Hays Medical Center, in Kyle, TX, the very next day. From there, I was transferred to a center for battered women. I was the lone adult male there, and I spent a month there.

I sure didn't think I would find myself here, or in another hospital bed with broken ribs again, or more trauma to an interesting turn of events. I left a lifestyle only to find more of the same lifestyle in an environment for battered women who have already gone through hell. I really understand why some people think that they are fucked for life, but as messed up as things were going, I was totally determined to get to Michigan; it was all I could think about. And I was going to make it happen, no matter what! In my short time in the Upper Peninsula of Michigan, or as the local natives, say there, da UP. Maybe it was the snow, I'm sure it was the clean water and friendly people I had met the first time around. Believe me, I clung to that impression during my month at that place in Central Texas. As drugs and drinking were rampant at the center, and believe me I was so tempted, but to hell with the idea that I'm fucked for life, I have never believed that since March 23 2003, when I tried to kill myself. I felt I survived for a reason, and I clung onto that. I don't know what kept the notion of traveling to Michigan burning in my brain, I mean that's all I could focus on during those trying times. Night after night that I stayed in that shelter, that is what kept me from joining the party again. Thanks to the wonderful impression that they left on me.

As I finally left Texas, I drove yet again from Texas to Michigan with high hopes, actually my only hope. There is a funny thing happening around the country at this very moment that is very difficult to explain. As I have traveled all over this country by this point, surface impressions are just that. To me, I felt all Catholics had deep convictions and beliefs. I mean you have to in order to practice the faith, but something is different, something palpable is happening to this faith as I write this. In my travels all over the heartland of America, there is a quiet movement that is concrete in its values and convictions, but it is not one of compassion and forgiveness. Let me illustrate what happened to me once I arrived in Michigan after a long arduous drive.

I left with two traveling companions from that shelter, one was a woman in her early 30s and her daughter, who also were sick of the conditions at the shelter. We made it to Michigan in late July of 2016, despite me having a few flashbacks and stopping in Omaha again for a conference at Bellwether. So I'm walking the walk, the best way I know how with nothing but making it to Michigan on my mind. I have no idea what to expect, other than the Catholic community was going to be great up there! (Or at least in my mind it was going to be). In my naivety, I had sent an email to the only contact I had made from a prayer group in Marquette, Michigan, stating that I was feeling so blessed to be heading that way. I didn't get much of a response, nor did my email really get forwarded to the priest at the church that I was requesting would get done. For whatever reason, I ended up driving to Marquette, MI, blind and not knowing anyone, but hey I'm fearless, convicted and faithful. Could you blame me? I had high hopes. I did place all my faith in God, for after all I've been through, I felt I came out on the other side for a reason. That is all I knew to be true.

I have heard it on a national news radio program of this term that people in a Minnesota call what I experienced in Michigan the first time, a term called 'Minnesota nice.' To my understanding as I heard some mid-westerners in my journeys, and as it was confirmed in this radio program I heard last week, was this: It is a term in which people in order to avoid outright confrontations, would be 'nice' to your face, but as soon as you turn your back, the truth comes out as far as what people discuss and think of race. Yes, no different than anywhere else on the planet, but I must confess, I grew up in Austin, Texas, and oh, how naive I was about the mood in my country. I figured that the days of racial bigotry were behind us all. I do feel compelled to write this because of the current situations harming our beautiful country as many people are marching on the streets as I write this. It is the Women's March to mark the one year anniversary of this administration. I write this to prove my conviction of how much God has changed me for the good. While I was married, I studied political science at Texas State University. Politics is a wonderful passion of mine, it has been since I was a teen. My divorce forced me to not continue my education, but in my very short academic stay in San Marcos, Texas, I do have a 3.0 GPA. So I know this 'gifted' boy can do the work, but I just haven't had the opportunity to finish my education. Maybe one day I will; as I write this, I have a deep respect and admiration for learning. (Kids: stay in school! I'll get off my soapbox). My point with this is that, good or bad, the only thing that matters to me is the Lord. I am exercising my free will to make very good decisions based on faith, love and mercy. Nothing else matters, not even the current racial or political pressures of the day. As I have stated before, I have the absolute grace to stride confidently with the ultimate joy of serving a very loving God. Believe me, every chance I get, I walk it like God talks it; meaning I am full of joy and love.

Am I perfect? Not at all! In fact, I am very flawed, yet I'm joyful.

That is the true beauty of the struggle for union with God.

So, here I enter this community. Most of these people here that hadn't ever seen a Latino or many of them in their lives. I know this because some of the residents there even came out to say it. I guess most people only know what they know from the idiot box (TV), but what do I know, I haven't owned one in three years. I hadn't even paid attention to the politics because you can pretty much read a headline and realize that not much changes in the realm of American politics. What is happening in America is rapidly alarming, but you know what I believe already; I know who has this firmly in His control. I don't fear even talk of an apocalypse or cataclysmic end.

There was a kind senior couple that took in myself and the woman and child I was traveling with. They let us stay with them for a few weeks as I got a job and found a place for us to rent as roommates, I felt I made it very obvious that this woman was only a friend, but to my consternation, that senior couple felt like I had obligations to her and the child. Please keep in mind that most of these people hadn't even gotten to know a Latino, much less and man traveling with a woman and child. I grew up in one of the most liberal cities in America, but that being said, this living situation was terse and tedious at best. Aren't we all on the same spiritual team, or at least the same stadium? My gosh, I was just about to get my crash course on whatever is this palpable, unspeakable tension that I feel is crippling this land at the moment. I feel like we're in an episode of the twilight zone, but not even that, it's more like the movie Twilight with people choosing sides like team Justin or Edward with the absurd notions that we cannot be dissenting into a chaotic melodrama played out on reality TV. But if we have truly lost our way as Americans, I have faith that we will find our way back to the true American spirit that this country was founded on. I have true faith in that. What I will not do is pick a side, when we are all children of God. I am done with meaningless vitriol, name calling and desire to be right. I'd rather be happy; that is my truth at this point as I entered Marquette, Michigan, on a spiritual high as opposed to other things that I have tried all my life. I hate starting a sentence with the conjunction, but that being said, we live in an age where everyone doubts more and God is less relevant. Let me qualify that statement that even the 'faithful,' a term that to me now is as useless as 'gifted,' or 'potential,' by my experience in Michigan. As I briefly alluded to early in this manuscript, there are two definitions of faith, complete trust in someone or something, or strong belief in doctrines or God. God is real to me, love is real to me, so it is essential to me to view God as a living breathing entity. True faith isn't walking a fine line and just following archaic rules, it is actually living your faith. It says so in a book that is now regulated as a work of fanciful virtues, called the Bible. What good is our faith if it is tired and weak, and doesn't stand for anything other than a social gathering to discuss polite issues and pleasantries. I have been to Catholic churches all over this beautiful country and I have seen it all, meaning this overwhelming reflection on self that is more self-centered than selfless, like our faith insists. There is a lack of reverence in our faith (I am only speaking on some churches, it is like a 50/50 split, but more perceptible in the Midwest than other areas of the country). Does this mean I am condemning or speaking heresy? I shall hope not. These are just observations. For example, in Iowa there was this church where I overheard women speaking in the tabernacle on how more people should speak English in this country. Now for my non-Catholic brothers and sisters, this is a very sacred place of the church where absolute reverence is expected, and silence is to be totally observed unless you are praying. In Oklahoma, there was a parish, where on a particular 9/11 observance the flag was brought out in front of the alter. It was held as if I were back in the boy scouts, and this priest didn't even give us a blessing and most observances were skimmed over and prayer was kept to a minimum. In Michigan there was more of the same, so I'm not saying everyone is like this, of course not, I am saying that there is a palpable difference in reverence as opposed to folks leaving before mass is over, or talking during mass, or wearing football jerseys and skimpy clothing to the house of God. So, I use the term 'faithful' with as loose of an interpretation as I feel. True faith can only be measured by God! And I will state this! My good actions far outweigh my rap sheet. But only God can judge me, but that is the irony. I know that if I weren't doing things the right way, that I wouldn't be so despised, and that to me is a true test of faith; believing when all the chips are down.

There are huge differences in parishes that have a sound foundation of faith, and in my humble opinion, between others that don't. Please keep in mind that I am not a theologian, just a very observant man that is on a journey to find healing. In the churches that I have felt my faith encouraged and accepted was one in Little Rock, Arkansas, where there was an obvious diversity, and for lack of a better word, spiritual connection, meaning there was silence, prayer and reflection. In Kyle, Texas, there was standing room only, even the tabernacle was full! There were folks who were new and you could tell. In another church in Texas, people were wearing their second hand best, like those vinyl shoes that crack when you walk, and it smelled of gasoline. I guarantee you that there wasn't a sports jersey in the house, and that it was also full. In Michigan, I went to two churches and there were two distinct differences that were very noticeable and definite.

I entered at the mercy of one of the aforementioned types of churches where there was a cliquish feel to it, where there was a defined status quo and things don't change much, and right or wrong, change of any type is frowned upon. I had just arrived there in July of 2016, on total emotional and financial fumes, so to speak. I was down to my last hundred dollars as I had anticipated getting a job and staying at a weekly motel just outside of Marquette, Michigan. I didn't go in totally blind, I had sent an email to a parishioner there at the church which I had hoped would reach the pastor there, but it did not, but I'm a resourceful guy. I went to church the next day with my traveling companion and her child. There is a blessing to extending and opening your doors to a new parishioner, and I was totally blessed with somewhere to call home and lay my head. A wonderful senior couple had taken us weary travelers in. To put this in perspective, I had been on the road since February 9 2016. I had been sleeping everywhere from beaches, parks, my car, sofas, women's abuse shelter and more hotels than I care to remember. I was so grateful for this couple's generosity. I had a running, warm shower, alone, without interruption, and I cried for the first time in tears of joy and thanksgiving. Unbeknownst to anyone there, I was right where I wanted to be, nor had anyone known what I had been through, as in my mind I was just there to heal. It was a fresh start for me, and that is all I cared about.

My many years of therapy, group meetings and psychoanalysis had shown me that because of my circumstances, I knew that I had a long road ahead of me for recovery. I also fully understood that only time could heal me. And I had a three part plan for myself which included the physical, mental and spiritual sides of myself. My truth and trinity, if you will. As the prevailing political winds changed in our country and hope turned into pride somehow, and insecurity and fear reign in the hearts of men, I soon found out that the free spirit that lies within me, and my freedom from my past life, would be such a struggle to maintain. So, the beauty and the irony of life sometimes is this! I was living in a two bedroom duplex, alone, because I didn't feel like the living situation I had planned with this woman and her child would just not work out for a variety of reasons; the main reason was that I couldn't give myself intimately to this woman, and she desired very much so to be with me. So little by little, I kept cutting anything or anyone that didn't either understand what I was doing, or was a negative influence in my life.

Oh, how my life changed when I started making more room for God in it, meaning drama, sex, drugs and dependence on others for validation, totally left me in every form. I was free and extremely joyful. I had always been compassionate and joyful, but this was different, for sure! As much as I wanted to be alone, people were curious as to who I was and why I was so joyful. It didn't compute in this cold calculated community that was no different than the 'good ol' boy' system in Texas. No one could understand how I was such a force of nature. Basically, I was just filled with the Holy Spirit after my lightening quick spiritual experience, and I just wanted to love everyone. In today's constant hustle and bustle, people rarely seem to take the time to say hello to each other, much less greet each other on the street. I had traveled much of the country at this point, and to this day it confuses me. From a metroplex in the Dallas/Ft. Worth area, with a population of over six million to Marquette, MI, with a population of about 21,000, the mood and the disconnect are obvious. And positivity and joy are looked upon as lunacy or the act of chemical addiction. I don't know how many times since that Pentecostal experience I have been asked if I was on drugs or told that I'm crazy. It ultimately made for a very lonely existence. I felt like I had to fight cynicism and detractors on an hourly basis.

The struggle began in earnest, with forces that are attacking the very fabric of our national identity. As we are failing to listen or understand each other. We as people are questioning our own identity and failing to see the 'Christ' in each other. We have become a nation that lives our lives in hyper speeds and no clear direction, again like myself that didn't stand for anything, therefore falling for everything. With the information age in full swing with our souls hanging in the balance and no clear objective, we are as weak as we ever have been. The joy comes from the struggle and overcoming adversity, that is what made America great in the first place, for example the great depression led to the creation of America's greatest generation, and a time that everyone can agree on, where the growth of the middle class and American prosperity generated many benefits for this nation. Imagine if our grandparents had been given pharmaceutical solutions to get through the greatest suffering our nation has ever known, or if our nation was told to go to therapy for every 'issue' we came across. Or that Elvis Presley should have been given something for his restless legs, only to have the true chemical solution for Elvis lead him to death on a toilet.

All kidding aside, I met a woman in Marquette, MI, who would forever change my life, and outlook on love. A woman who is truly graceful in my eyes, and whom has had the greatest challenges thrown at her in this life as well. Are we a nation of compassion or self-pity? This is the question we have to ask ourselves as we struggle to find ourselves as we are in a war for our souls. To be or not to be, that is the question? As any great romance starts out, with the proverbial, 'I wasn't looking for a relationship…and then it happened,' actually happened to me in the most unexpected place farthest from any semblance of home and in my most free state of being. Meaning that for the first time in my life, I was experiencing myself as I was intended to be; free from dysfunction and independent of anyone. I was living my faith and entering a new spiritual awakening inside the very depths of my soul.

As I reflect on my time in Michigan and the 'new' love in my life, I am reminded of what it means to be a friend, and that is what my best friend taught me. In a world where everyone had abandoned me and the only woman to show me true friendship and trust, I had new skills to embark on in my next foray into love, but I was not ready. Remember I have PTSD and major depression, and all of this had just been accurately diagnosed for the first time in my life. With this beautiful mother of eight, I am faced with new challenges along with being faithful in my new spiritual experiences. Life has a way of throwing all manner of challenges, especially when one is newly convicted with faith the world isn't the same. I have had many profound experiences in my life, and it seemed to me that I either dismissed them or fell short of trying to maintain some progress when all crap hit the fan. The nuance of the spiritual life as I am learning does require a great deal of self-control and faith. It is 2016, and I am struggling to remember how to pray a rosary. I didn't even know the new mysteries of light or the Apostle's Creed. When I initially started to come back to my faith as I understood it, I could only recite the Sorrowful Mysteries and that is all I could do. I prayed that was good enough for Mother Mary. I knew how flawed I was and still am. I was not concerned about doing it right, I was desperate for solutions to the alleged rape of my daughter, my own lost innocence and that bastard loneliness. I was in Michigan to heal, and here is this wonderful family in adoration with me.

This woman is a mother of eight children who has been divorced for six years. She has been a single mother dealing with raising little treasures in a faith that I know saves firsthand. That is the tie that binds her and me…our faith. We met on a Tuesday afternoon, during adoration in a church just outside of Marquette, MI. I had just found out that my father was diagnosed with esophageal cancer, and I had just met with the priest there. I had just spent an hour there. For my non-Catholic brothers and sisters, that is a place in either the tabernacle or the alter, where the Eucharist is exposed for our faithful to adore. If you haven't spent time there, believe me, something happens. For example, I remember that my mom started to bring me sometime after my separation from my wife in or around 2013 or so. And believe me, I sat there in the tabernacle and just tapped my foot for an hour. And I thought I wasn't feeling anything, but here I was some time later, going of my own free will, and spending some time there. The first time I was coming down off of some chemicals or some absurd binge and my mom was exasperated at my behavior, I sat there ultimately feeling stupid for resisting such a serene and reverent observance. Fast forward a few years, and I'm literally spending as much free time as I could at the tabernacle. If I have aroused anyone's curiosity, take it from me, just go. It took years, but I clearly had that mustard seed type of belief, either that, or I was just beaten into total submission in this life. Like I have mentioned many times, I am not a theologian, so I am not qualified to answer the technicalities of how this works. I think I finally just accepted what the term mystery of faith is. I don't have the most logical answers, but this is a book about faith.

To continue my love journey, or hopefully it's ending destination, some weeks later while I was working at my job for a shoe retailer, I noticed a beautiful woman and her daughter staring at me with the most amused comical look on their faces as I was dancing on a ladder to the song 'Sir Duke' by Stevie Wonder. I make a fool of myself on a daily, if not regular basis, so I don't think it weird when others look at me that way. But I did immediately step down from the ladder and immediately walked over to them. I immediately recognized them as the family from that church outside of Marquette. The woman and her oldest daughter that were there praying at adoration, were quizzically staring at me. I introduced myself and found myself comfortable enough to discuss dating with the then 13-year-old daughter. I mean the immediate audacity of a total stranger in a strange land, discussing topics that I later found was offending every bit of this young lady's sensibility. It is totally amazing to see quickly how compatible two people can be together when the most unlikely of temperaments and upbringing are brought together by the cosmos, or whatever you may choose to call it. What I didn't expect was that this woman and I would fall deeply in love, and when the random meeting in adoration turns into a not so random meeting at my job! I knew this had to be investigated, even though I was in Michigan to heal. And of course, we ended up meeting for coffee at a local coffee shop shortly afterward. The fact that this wasn't technically a date because she presented it to me as a business opportunity that could 'change' my life. I was naturally curious to find out, but truth be told, I thought she was hot. I reflect back to my childhood and remember having crushes on various Catholic schoolgirls, like that Red Hot Chili Pepper's song goes, they rule!

Please keep in mind that I've been single for three years, and I enjoyed my bachelor lifestyle and really didn't want the complication of a relationship after such a rough and tumble marriage. I especially wasn't going to get involved with another woman who had children (eight of them!), and embark on another whirlwind of a love affair as I had so many times in my life. Immediately, I was faced with the indecision and insecurity that comes with a new beginning (And did I mention eight kids?). There was that undeniable mystical force at work, a power greater than us bringing us together. As if the timing, planets, and all that other malarkey brought us to that point in that coffee shop on the pretense of a business opportunity that would have life changing implications, for both of us. All kidding aside, we never talked about the business. We shared stories of laughter and pain, we comforted each other as we came to know each other's pain and rejection from the world. And to think that we shared the same faith! That for me, was the no-brainer, or at least a grand foundation.

I had no blueprint for a relationship, all I had was an avalanche of failed attempts. With misguided forays of love imitated from bad 80s movies. Or like a John Hughes epic classical comedy where Duckie finally gets his girl, or am I the cowardly lion? Hell no! I am just going to assume that everyone reading by now, is familiar with the Catholic view on chastity and abstinence from sex until marriage, so I believe that there is no need to elaborate. This is a novel idea for me, one that friendship had always been screwed up by sex. As I have explained about myself, I'm a man who lives passionately and has experienced all manner of pleasure, and somehow had still felt a void in my life. I have to preface all of this because it seems to me that everyone lately looks at life through a manner of a purely black and white lens, and I'm not talking about race, yet! I'm speaking in terms of right and wrong. There is what is right and clearly what is wrong, but a man or woman's heart can be good, yet they do wrong in the eyes of the law or court of public opinion. We all consistently judge, and I don't care really what anyone says or judges me on what I'm about to write. I truly believe that I am set free, and also truly believe that if Mary Magdalene were alive today, she'd be stoned to death no matter who stood in the way. It is sad to say that an angel could be right in front of my face, and I'm so jaded I wouldn't even acknowledge its presence. That is how closed my heart was, and I am reminded of how my best friend in life taught me the meaning of friendship.

This a reflection and a very personal story about my best friend in life, and someone whom I love more than my own family, and the ultimate litmus test of toxicity and health, a fair comparison of love and lust, and real and not so genuine people. What I mean by this, is that there is such a thing as wrong or right, when it comes to relationships, lifestyles, or friendships. They must have a foundation of love and honesty. I find that if I keep things simple and focused on the present moment, I can discern a certain truth and of course, hindsight is the best way to reflect on things. To truly learn, I must admit at first that I make mistakes. I guess this is where my rearview mirror is oh so useful and less confusing when I look at my life with forgiveness and mercy on myself. I met my true partner in crime shortly after my separation from my wife. I struggled with myself for a long time about whether or not I should include this in this narrative, and after much deliberation with loved ones, I feel that times like this call for full disclosure and truth. I know that I will be judged, but in all honesty, I am not ashamed. I just know what works for me. After my separation, I encountered a loneliness that many divorced individuals are quite familiar with. And after my struggles with early family and desire for love, I went out and sought it through my life's normal vices. I feel pertinent need to mention this because my best friend and I were inseparable for many, many years. I met her in a drunken response to a personal ad for a threesome.

This wasn't the first one I had been in, but this was the first one where the woman was not really a woman, she was transgendered. I will not get into the gender identity politics that is being played today, but I do have much love and respect for the LGBTQ community. I understand when a person says that coming out gave them the courage to be who they are, it actually gives me a lot of courage to be who I am in my faith, so this is a kiss to being who you are! For some reason, there was something electric between us; we couldn't take our eyes off of each other. There was a gentleness to our intimacy and her boyfriend was the proverbial third wheel. This is why I believe that no couple, gay or straight, should engage in threesomes in order to enhance a lackluster romance. I have only met one couple who could do this and they were gay men who had been together 17 years (There are unconventional attitudes to all rules and obtuse ways thinking on relationships). If I have any critique on the lifestyle of the LBGTQ community, it is the lack of long lasting relationships that I have observed in my many years of having many, many dear friends in it.

What I am saying in truth, is the lack of longevity in a lot of relationships, even in heterosexual ones. Many are fueled by the emotion and lack of trust in experiences that these relationships breed. For example, I feel that when sex becomes a power struggle, it is actually filled with a lack of substance and the mere act of sex is just that, an act. I have the credibility to say this because of the nature of one of the most beautiful loves I have ever experienced was with my best friend. At that time, I was hurting incredibly intensely and seeking companionship at any level, it didn't matter to me if she had a penis or not. The story of us initially started out with lust, but something real happened in this encounter. I immediately went searching for the same experience of intimacy that was intense. But aye there is the rub, in a community swept up by an identity crisis, masked by alcohol and drug use, it is no wonder I got swept into that lifestyle. I met another transgendered woman with whom I had a great time with, but again, I was trying to replicate that same intimacy I had encountered with my best friend, but to no avail; I didn't find it. I was at the club with this young woman, and I saw my future best friend there. What a coincidence, but I really don't believe in it. Things happen for a reason, I survived for a reason and we all have a reason. It's Satan's lie that tells us we don't. What I know about the devil, is that he has no soul, on the other hand I do. I have a lot of love to give no matter how much I have been hurt or put through adversity. What I want most is a relationship, for when my looks fade and my junk doesn't work anymore, that my partner and I still have something fulfilling. I believe that could be true for anyone.

It didn't take long for my best friend and me to realize that we weren't sexually compatible, in part to our last sexual encounter. Now, I absolutely hate car sex. I hate all the maneuvering involved and the seats are never comfortable enough, but one does make exceptions when he believes he is in love. My bestie and I were high as kites and proceeding to have the act of sex, but something was different in this, our last encounter. Some can or will say it was the drugs and alcohol, but as this illustration will show, we grew out of this need to be intimate. What the deciding factor for me in most intimate situations is the amount of sensuality that I need in an encounter. For example, if I don't feel that my partner isn't enjoying it, I don't mind stopping the whole production. Sex has to have a genuine attraction, safety, comfort, trust and love, as I have grown in my appreciation of sex as something more than an act. My bestie and I came to a crossroads in the appreciation of ourselves and respect for each other.

What ensued in this car mishap was that there was a dominance that came across in her sex that was distinctly different from that first time and clearly rubbed me wrong. There was no sensuality, in fact, it was very power driven and full of vulgarity that most in the community embrace as role play, or more of a submissive or dominant roles, hence the lust and power that I referenced earlier. I mean is Fifty Shades of Grey really a glamorization of brutal violence in our sex? Since when have sex and violence been synonymous? I guess in less civilized times, but aren't the ways of the past coming back in a huge way, such as the brutalization of sex. In our advanced intelligence, how can we resort to barbaric ways of denigration and dereliction? I don't know how many times she called me a bitch or cum slut, but I jumped out of the car and in anger I crushed our pipe and dumped out the drugs. I am vehemently opposed to this treatment of myself by someone I loved. I called her all kinds of names, and she just looked at me with bewilderment. That situation for me was eye opening because there was an easy trap for someone as wounded as me to fall into. For me, that dangerous mix of thinking I am in control or surrendering my control, then basing my entire love life on that. I have never been comfortable with a woman being totally submissive to me. Something like that dominance and aggression leads to a diluted form of passion for me and the act becomes just an exercise in futility. What scares me about our culture's obsession with sex and violence, is that usually people get hurt, both emotionally and physically. It is way too easy to get carried away during the passion of sex. After my exposure to what certain men pay for, it is no wonder why our lines of decency have been blurred and confused.

After that moment in the car things were different for us, and we had commenced on a friendship that would last for years. I could go on for chapters of the ups and downs that most friendships go though. I could glorify the number of times we had fun, but one point that I want to glorify is love and acceptance. We vowed not to speak of this with anyone, and we kept our silence until I wrote this. There were times in our friendship that we loved, laughed, fought and cried harder than most married couples ever feel in a lifetime, and that isn't an exaggeration. The fact is, we always came back to each other. There wasn't a day that went by that we didn't at least check in with each other, and that was the closest friend I have ever had in my life. She was the closest person I had to family in my entire life. I learned how to be a good friend, how to walk, talk and ooze confidence. I found my voice when I met her, and she fell in love for the first time at the age of 31. I would say that we both made each other better people. For a man that has had his closest family betray him, it could've been easy to stay in the lifestyle that is very passionate and fun, but again I started this memoir about a search for love and truth, and I am still searching for something to fill this void at this point. This brings me back to one of my main points of trying to maintain faith and being faithful in a world that is so filled with detours and pitfalls.

As I mentioned at the start of this book, my dad had just passed from esophageal cancer, but at this moment that I met my new friends, I had just recently found out about his diagnosis. I was bitterly torn apart about giving a damn in the first place, I really didn't care about who saw my tears, but in this instance I was. I saw this beautiful family staring at me with a compassionate curiosity. I must admit, I was intrigued. But I had crusty mucus on my dark pants and I was self-conscious about my tears. I genuflected, which is a form of praise and respect, by kneeling. I walked out of adoration and proceeded to my job.

At this point in my spiritual journey, I'm meeting huge obstacles like learning to trust, surrender and the disciplines required of even going to church every day. I met the challenges head first with unshakable faith, like a child. The faith that I had as a child was oh so necessary, to maintain some semblance of stability in a life less than ordinary. I had to have faith or else I would succumb to the madness of my victimhood, and I hate playing the victim in any capacity because I had literally been on my own since I was 16, when my dad kicked me out of the house at that tender part of my life; all I had known was to be resourceful and survive. But man does not live on bread alone, right? It seems to me that man does not live on sex, drugs, more sex, and lots of drugs either. Outside of having a million dollar trust fund, I guess if I had been brought up in a more privileged environment I could've been president of the United States, but it is so easy to pick on a man; he is too easy of a target. I have grace in this graceless age, and this is how I did it.

Every day, I would get up and go to mass, then I would exercise, next I would work and I would heed my spiritual advisors suggestions. I stayed in constant prayer and ate much healthier. I limited people who drained me of my precious little energy, and I know I came off as rather stand offish and curt when I met new people at church. No one knew what pain I carried or what kind of struggle it was just to get out of bed in the morning, but I was damned if I was going to go down the gamut again of psych meds and group therapy sessions where I was limited to what I could talk about, and quite frankly, yoga and mantras didn't do it for me. The things that humbled me, were the things I was oh so scared of, and change seemed so uncomfortable. If my life hadn't taught me anything by now, then I was never going to learn and quite frankly, I was desperate. Here was a woman who had spent the last six years being a single mother and working, and she chose me because I nudge her out of her comfort zone. Now is that an all-time pick up line? How come I didn't think of that? I pray I never have to use another line to pick up another woman again. Herein lies the conundrum. Am I too jaded by the world to see a good woman when she is right in front of me? We're like oil and water, night and day, shy and outgoing, or whatever opposite you want to apply to this old adage. But like magnetism, they do attract and something electric happens. My problem is trusting this new love, and a million fears crop up. The meaningless vices brought me to my knees, in a literal sense of course, because I hit those most mornings to give thanks for just being alive.

So, here comes this new relationship that is oh so enticing for the both of us, and we are grappling with the normal getting to know you stuff. She's chalked full of fear as well; she had been married and hurt for sixteen years, I was having trouble just being me, and again what we had in common was our faith. Blessed the one, who sees the forest for the trees, right? I'm at a new parish, barely finding my faith, and I'm a prickly pear because I don't let many people get next to me. I have long hair at this point and tattoos. A priest actually asked me rhetorically if I knew that I looked different from most people around there in Michigan. He also questioned the pope and cursed in his office, I think that took me more by surprise though. I had grown up in Austin, Texas for over 20 years, and I thought this type of thinking had passed, but again I am a stranger in a strange land, so I don't really want to rock the boat. Plus, by growing up in Texas, I'm not a stranger to that subtle racism. It's all good, because the only way I was taught to get past it was to prove them wrong, but this new place seemed like a time warp to the fifties in the most digressive ways. You could leave your doors unlocked at night, and for the most part you were safe. Yet, the obtuse thinking and narrow mindset was rampant. My new love and I had been dating for a few months, and a close friend of hers had managed to pull a background check on me. She brought a copy of it to my new girlfriend and presented her with my criminal background. I was proverbially flabbergasted because my privacy had been violated and my past sins used against me in a way to convince my girlfriend that I was a monster, but to my credit, I had already come clean with her about my past. The truth had truly set me free in this instance and gave me the inspiration to begin writing. My beautiful angel told her close friend at the time that I had already informed her of my former life, and that it was a pity that no one took the time to get to know me there at the parish. A lot of people had pity for my girlfriend at the time, but I believe it was exactly that, pity, not true compassion, because instead of being happy for her, we encountered a bunch of resistance and we were ostracized to the point we had to switch churches.

This switch in churches is a small, yet poignant, microcosm of how fractured our country is at the moment. For example, my closest male friend in Michigan had been a third of fourth degree Knight of Columbus. We became good friends at church, and he helped me get settled with some furniture in my new place in a town just outside of Marquette. This man was also divorced, and we would spend the weekends together keeping each other company. I had placed my trust in a man for the first time in a long time. I became vulnerable and let someone in. I shared my thoughts and feelings with another man, and I thought because he shared the same faith and was a Knight of Columbus, just like I am that it was safe. Again, I placed my hopes in finding a true friend, but things changed on one of those nights when we had a discussion about race and politics. Couple that with me crying in his arms during a flashback, and his inner man came to the forefront shortly after. I guess I had fallen into a friendship because he gave me furniture, or companionship. We had even worked in the church garden to grow pumpkins for the upcoming Halloween celebration for the church. I thought it was safe to be open and honest, but herein lies the issue that is emblematic of the divide in our country. During our last spirited conversation, he was going to show me something online where he referred to black men dancing in a line as 'monkeys.' I simply made a statement that was not cool to say. This man became enraged and belligerent as he defended himself as not being a racist for saying that. This man lived with a lot of repressed frustration, I know this because we had many discussions about his sufferings. Life is too short for me to hold on to any resentments, so I pray that he finds some comfort. I suspect that we as men live with too much repressed anger that seems to be the common observation that I have witnessed in my travels and experiences. It could also explain why I don't let many men into my life.

By stark contrast, my girlfriend was being shown a very different kind of charity, by her next-door neighbor. This man was also her landlord, whose charity will always remain in my heart. My girlfriend had her run of misfortune with an ex-husband who would've made my ex-wife proud. Her ex-husband hadn't paid child support in seven years. As it stands to this day, he is well over ten thousand dollars in arrears in financial support for his children. For a single mother of eight, that presents a set of unreal challenges for anyone, religious or not. My girlfriend had raised those children on her own and was allowed to live in her home rent free for over a year by her current neighbor. He wouldn't accept a dime from her. That is a man I can respect for sure! He is the kind of man I aspire to be. He's a professor at Northern Michigan University there in Marquette. He lives with great passion, and we both share a love for wine. He reminded me of some great friends back in Austin, Texas. For example, one day we gave him a ride to his home as he was walking back from the university. Never mind that the temperature was in the mid-twenties, he was wearing a kilt. He hopped on the side runners of the truck we were in and rode the rest of the way to his home. I mention all of this because I have heard our pope say that some agnostics will get into heaven as opposed to some that go to church on Sunday. I am definitely not one to judge, it is way above my pay grade, but the professor was an agnostic. Who are we to say who has a true loving heart, but I do know that actions are louder than words. I believe that this man acted out of love and lived free.

Being faithful when the chips are down, and maintaining faith are key to maintaining understanding, wisdom and some form of sanity. The road was getting oh more difficult when people of faith are failing to maintain open hearts and minds, because of a watered down belief in the ideals and virtues that made our faith last for thousands of years. I keep asking myself, is it the political climate? Is it the perverse nature of old uncivilized ways creeping back into our way of living? I believe that what made our nation great was a beautiful combination of Judaism and Christianity. Does anyone remember one nation under God? I'm not speaking of morality, I'm speaking of ethics and by definition they are different. That is why there is a separation of church and state. Here's another idea while I have the podium: keep sex separate too. Keep it out of my politics, it gets in the way of my freedom of religion. I am OK with whatever one wants to do in their bedroom, believe me it is above my pay grade to judge what anyone does. I'm a father, not a drug dealer, pimp, addict or sex fiend. I'm just a man who is upset about the condition in what we are leaving this planet to future generations. As a nation, we are all about family values and such, but we have no compassion for a mother raising eight children on her own for six years. I want my children to come to their own truths without nearly as many trials and tribulations that most of us have to go though, just to come down to the plain simplicity that we all want to love and be loved. In the example of this woman I just met, the community felt sorry of her, but was hardly happy with her decision to date me. Nor were they willing to embrace her children as I so clearly did. I actually put my money where my mouth and desire was, and I spent every day with them. Now, the world questions my sanity on a daily basis and that is OK with me, but I'll be lost forever if I don't embrace fully what I have been so scared to faithfully try. I don't believe in the term born again virgin, but I do fully set my pride aside to try a new way of living and respect for a woman who has been through nearly as much as me. She makes me happy, and I don't care what anyone else says.

One can only imagine the conversations that took place in this small town. The struggle between liberalism and extreme conservative ideology was waging in full force for all to see. I worked at a coffee shop, and the day after the election of 2016 things were different, but still the same. Some were in a deep state of hopelessness, some were gloating, some felt that the fix was in, some didn't care, and I was with the latter. I am a passionate man and one who had paid attention to politics all my life. I voted in every election since I was 18, I'm very civic-minded. I didn't vote. I conscientiously objected and I caught flak for it. To the ultra-conservative, I was unpatriotic. To the liberal I was part of the problem, and I didn't help them win. Here is my stance, and I will hold fast to this until America gives us a candidate that represents the true identity of us all: I'm calling for someone that respects life, is conservative with our economy, tough on crime, has vision, and true compassion for all people. Until then, I will write in Jesus on my ballot because we are the greatest nation this world has ever seen, and I know we have brilliant minds either man or woman that can carry our nation for another two hundred years. But alas, I am searching for love and trust, not brownie points for insights that have been exhausted on any news channel that you turn on.

So, this is the environment that I had to travel back to Texas in; a nation divided, and everyone up in arms and accusing each other like we are not the America I grew up with in the nineties. My new relationship had to be put on hold and two things were tested in which I had little to no faith in; long distance relationships or my ability to trust anyone. I left Michigan with way more questions than answers in my journey, and I had to deal with my dying father whom had lost consciousness from his cancer surgery. From the moment I flew in from Michigan, I was driven to the airport, and I was immediately faced with my dying father. I couldn't believe that I was there, and I couldn't believe that I gave a damn in the first place. I hadn't seen my dad in three years or so, and our relationship was essentially nonexistent.

Our last encounter was violent and my exact last words to him were, "Why don't you try fucking yourself!" To which he said nothing. In the three instances in which I had mentioned my abuse to him, he never even denied it, in fact, he was very abusive and didn't let my own mom speak to me for a couple of years. So, if my mom and I did speak, she had to text or call when he wasn't around. I had no idea what I was doing there, but I knew that the aforementioned statement of profanity couldn't be the last words he heard me say. I had a whole script in my mind as to what I was going to say, but that went out the window as soon as I saw him. He was unconscious, both lungs were aspirated, and he had pneumonia. My mother was in such paralytic fear and sadness, I couldn't figure it out. I never saw my sister there. She didn't want to see me, then it occurred to me that my mother was just spread too thin and in total disarray about the dissolution of her dream, which was to have a family. There were a bunch of wounds that were just open for the entire world to see. I initially wasn't going to stay too long, but my father ended up in the ICU for 33 days. I don't care what anyone says, but no one deserves to suffer like that. Maybe he did, but that isn't what I truly believe. My emotions teetered and went all over the map like a chaotic

System of a Down song. My sadness was there for the entire hospital to see and what was meant to be a week stay was actually an almost nine month odyssey that was just meant being away from this relationship that I had just started, but in my mind there were two things that I couldn't at the time abide by and that was a long distance relationship and faith in love. At this point, I was completely drained of love or compassion. It came down to a matter of faith, for me. I truly believe in love and mercy. I have to believe in that, or else my suffering would've been for nothing.

At this point in my life, I could've been justified at committing a murder, and I would have been treated like a king in prison, and that is the equivalent of being king of the dip shits. I say this because when I found out about all of the hurts in my life, I have considered killing those involved. It's a natural emotion when crimes of this sort of hurt, but I have been told by others that know about my situation that they would've killed all those involved. When I faced that choice, I knew one thing; I hate jail so much, no one is worth my freedom, so I'm willing to try this forgiveness thing! Back in 2015, in a Plano, TX, treatment center, which happened to be my last inpatient stay, I held onto a book about forgiveness for my entire two week stay. I learned about forgiveness from an 18-year-old woman named Dallas who led with an almost naïve pathos to forgive those who hurt her. I took her lead on something I knew nothing about, which was to start to let go. I'm not sure if she even let go of the crap she went through, but I started to let stuff go in 2015, and my life has taken a three plus year road to freedom. I wasn't about to lose my progress at this point. Nor was I about to hold on to this meaningless hate and anger that journeyed with me all my life. I had to stand up for what I believed in; mercy and love. That is what is at the core of the Catholic faith if you really look at it. I can't afford to complicate anything in my life, so I just let go again and whispered my last words to my father. It was a very complicated night for him. He fought his machines, the staff, the medicine and life in general.

Here is a man, who at the end of his life fought everything and anyone, and all I could think of to whisper in his ear was, "It's your son, I'm here now. We're men, and we don't need to talk about anything. If I have ever done anything to hurt you, I ask for your forgiveness." In his unconsciousness, he let out a few tears, and he stopped his fighting. He passed sometime after that.

In that act alone, a man was able to somewhat die in peace, and even if I hate him, I couldn't bear to see him die that way. Thirty-three days of utter hell on earth. The truth is, I thought he got off easy. That is at the core of my inner conflict as I still deal with awful flashbacks of what he did to me. I have a lifetime of crap to overcome such as intimacy, trust and my own emotional control. However, I do have less anger in my heart, and room for love. Plus, I maintain my commitment to write and share with others that may have gone through something like this, or any hurt in life, that there is a way out. Have I seen the light? Do I hold the keys to the kingdom? Am I a saint? The answer to all of that is has no clear answer, but I can say for a fact that I finally stood for something. And I'm done kicking my own ass. I have to believe that I am forgiven for my sins, and that no sin is bigger than God. So that being said, I have to forgive as I wish to be forgiven. I have to believe that or I'm not free. I would be a slave to regret, remorse, shame, and I wouldn't have the moxie to do anything in this life.

How does it all work? I have no clue, but I write this to illustrate that there are some universal truths in all of this. That if a man like me can be forgiven and set free, what could it mean for more righteous folk? It is presumptuous to think that my small act of self-preservation could help a soul get into heaven, but that is something I have to believe. But I can say that my father died a little easier, that is a fact. As Saint Pope John Paul II says, "Mercy is the solution to all of the world's problems."

I completely believe that. I have begun to remove myself out of the equation and make more room for good things in my life. I let go of the unforgiving and grudge filled ways of the world. The fruits of that remain to be seen, but anyone who knows me, or talks with me, knows that I am a very joyful, passionate and a loving man, even in my darkest sin. To further illuminate this testimony of my life, I will quote from a book called The Way of Humility written by a Cardinal Jorge Mario Bergoglio back in 2005. I am reminded of a prayer I had way back in 2006, when I asked God for humility, Oh my! What a sense of humor God has! This bares mention because for me, there wasn't much difference between being humiliated or being humbled, but regardless of point of view, if I remove my ego from the equation then God has more room to work. How often in this memoir have you read how I did everything, but allow God into my life? (I digress) The quote from this book comes from a footnote in it on page 35 that elaborates on the lack of shame in our society:

"Perhaps, a comparison may help us to understand this. Stealing a woman's purse is a sin, and the thief is sent to prison, and the woman tells her friends all about it, and everyone agrees that things are in a terrible state and that the public authorities ought to do something about it, because it is not safe to go out. And the woman in question, who has her purse snatched, never even thinks about what her husband is like in business matters, how he cheats the state by not paying taxes, gets rid of his employees every three months to avoid dependency in employment relations, and so on. And her husband, and perhaps she herself, boasts about these business tricks and underhanded dealings. This is what I call acceptable shamelessness. Another instance: prostitution is a sin, and prostitutes are called 'women of evil life' or simply 'bad women.' Socially, they are reviled for contaminating culture and corrupting people, et cetera, et cetera. And the same person who says all that, goes to a party for the third marriage of a friend (after the friend's second divorce) or accepts that so-and-so has a few 'affairs' (provided that they are in good taste) or that this or that film star's love life is published, when the star changes 'partners' like a pair of shoes. What I am getting at, is that there is a difference between the prostitute and this so-called liberal minded woman. The prostitute has not lost her shame: the other woman has gone beyond modesty and shame, and her attitude is one of shamelessness, which social convention makes acceptable."

Now, let me express what moved me about this footnote and why it was so important to me in this wonderful book. The subject matter of the former cardinal's book is this to me, that sin and corruption are not synonymous. What this means in the illustration and purpose of my writing is to show that I am a sinner for sure, but the whole time my heart wasn't corrupted. Therefore, hanging on to my hate would surely have closed my heart and I would definitely end up in the morgue, or worse yet, a spiritual death where I would be no good to anyone but me. I'll be damned if I will live like that. I would also lose my effectiveness as a servant of God, by not being a positive force in the world and to those around me. My dad was consumed by anger and envy. He envied me for becoming a better man than him, and as I came to find out, he was abused by his father as well. All I knew, is that I had to do everything opposite of him, and I did that. The cycle of abuse ends with me. The belief that the world is corrupt and that sin is acceptable is exactly why we are in the predicament in this day and age. We have accepted sin as a way of life and let ourselves be corrupted. It is as if I let myself accept that I was an alcoholic, therefore nothing would change. I would live life in the narrow scope of a twelve step program of my choice, and believe me, I can carry a membership card to any of them. If I settled into my victim stance of being a rape victim, I could justify my sexual behavior any way I wanted to because I was hurt and angry. If I settled for a life in crime, I could justify that life handed me a bad hand, and I have to live my life by the bluff of the rush of the crime. Meaning that there is a sense of satisfaction in committing crime, and being reviled. I can almost rationalize anything, and in the end everyone knows that rationalization is a lot like masturbation; in the end you're only screwing yourself! Thanks to my faith, I can honestly say that I am free from that bullshit of sin, therefore my heart is good. My shortcomings are numerous, my crimes are in my permanent file for all to see because it is public record, just like the tattoos on my arms. I am judged and vilified in some circles because I don't pray like others. I am talked about and gossiped on for my past actions, and I accept that because my crimes were many. I guess I deserve it, but I don't care. I am free. That is a fact. Sat Nam, people! My story is no different from that of anyone else. We all struggle with something. If there is something else I know for a fact, it is that there is joy in the struggle and peace in the pain. And it lies in the perfect acceptance in the fact that I am human, despite what my church mates think of me. Or despite what anyone else thinks of me. I know that people will balk at reading of my inner freedom, and most will look at ways to discredit my truth, but again I live and love for God and God alone. I reiterate that because it is true. And I truly live the golden rule to the best of my ability.

"Love your neighbor as yourself" (my father included). Love; that is the rub! The true test of a man or woman is the ability to love. I must avoid all things that close my heart to that one thing that this world needs most; love. I get laughed at so much from church to the streets when I mention that. It must be a sign of the times.

From politics to religion, we have been conditioned to close our hearts because we get watered down versions of the truth. From news, to music, to film. This same distortion of truth gets perpetuated. In the end, we are only diluting ourselves because we are filled with so much doubt as to who we are. The purpose of our lives is to love our neighbor, whether they are gay or straight, convicted or gossipers, faithful or faithless. I don't get it when people of my faith gossip, judge, or live in fear. The purpose of my life is to help another person; that is it! I knew that even in Dallas, Texas, way back in 2015! I'm a creature of love, not perfection. Love is rarely perfect, there are perfect moments, never perfect lives. Life is mucky and full of colors, not just black and white. Our closed hearts have fell prey to the lie that we don't need anyone or anything as long as we are gratified within seven to ten business days, or in six easy payments of whatever credit worth I obtain to show how worthy I am. I'm fun size, but I walk like I'm 6' 2", 220 pounds, and strong like The Rock. This is the final nail in the coffin of my old life. I may fall from grace, but the difference is I know what life without grace is, and that scares me beyond belief. I know I will suffer more. I know that I may suffer worse, but that will not shake my faith. My children may hate me, I may never get married again. Or I may get married again and divorce. Who knows what the future may have in store, but I guarantee that if I have held on thus far, I can handle whatever else comes my way. I am not your average cookie cutter Catholic, I'm one that understands Buddha, respects Allah, and loves as many people as I can. And I believe in one nation under God. That is what made us great in the first place. A nation that rejoiced in compassion and service. A nation that truly loved their children, more than sex or guns. I believe in a nation that should insure everyone medically, like we are forced to insure our vehicles, hell, I was Bernie Sanders before he came out of his crotchety closet. I don't give an empty compliment these days, nor do I gossip. I am very reverent when I go to church, and I don't miss a single Sunday. I pray a bunch, and I have very few regrets. I did more drugs than William Burroughs, and I lived to tell about it, but I won't give it too much glorification; that I save for God. For it was Him that saved me, yes, I said Him. Forget this gender identity or lack of it, because that is for the extreme liberal crazies to divide us. And those ultra conservative blowhards that can do no wrong and pervert our faith with an almost exclusive right to salvation, should stay out of my faith, because there is a separation of church and state that worked for over two hundred years for a reason. I will never put a pro-life sticker on my automobile because I won't politicize my beliefs anymore, instead I choose a rosary and I'm not shy about it. I tell people that I will pray for them because I will and do. I have example after example of answered prayer from almost miraculous to the tiniest of gratitude to God. But here I am, a man of love, on the high horse of criticism as I have in this work of storytelling, but alas, I leave it in to show my shortcomings are still there. This is the truth for me. I bare all of my insecurities and shortcomings, because it is the way I have always protected myself. If I get attacked by people about my shortcomings, I know for a fact that you are not a genuine friend.

While my life may be up for debate, my faith most certainly cannot be questioned. And as I sit here making important life changes for myself according to my faith as practiced and preached with love and mercy, I live my life to the fullest these days, being ever so careful not to hurt anyone in the process. I take the focus off of myself and expect nothing, and I am always blessed. My truth and choice lie within a kiss with a woman that is a mother of eight. That the world would say I am crazy for getting involved with as I embark on a new stage in my personal journey, but the truth is she makes me a better person. I'm a father first and foremost, and I truly enjoy being a dad. For some reason, I have been blessed with an average gift of playing guitar over the past three years, along with over one hundred rough musical compositions that have somehow been coming out as I write this narrative. Who knows if I will ever play them publicly, but the point is I am making proper choices with my free will. I am choosing to practice my faith more. I am choosing to make the riskiest venture in my life and that is to open my heart, yet again to a woman. This time with God being the focal point of our existence. With this choice, comes the responsibility of being accountable to another human, being vulnerable, and as you have read, honest. Lord willing, I will be on a beach with my guitar, singing, dancing and drinking a Mai Tai.

However, if life were as beautiful as a wedding in Central Park in April, things would have ended there. I know I would love to end this manuscript on a second marriage that lasted forever to this wonderful woman that had been through hell and back. Little did I know, that the ghosts of someone else's Christmas past would destroy this marriage of six months. It is two days prior to New Year's Eve, and this new marriage was sabotaged by yet another man's actions of sexual molestation, but this time it happened to my new bride. How is one to calculate such a cold desertion of yet another marriage to a woman with children whom I truly love to this day, I hold them very dear to my heart, yet I could not bring myself to sacrifice my broken heart and make it work for them, should I? Now one may ask, how come?

I can only offer what betrayal feels to someone who has been betrayed since birth by the man who was to show me how to live, acclimate to this thing called life, and prepare me for the pitfalls of adulthood and integrity. I want to truly address dishonesty and some of its shadowy friends. I think that we all can come to a consensus that omissions are lies. This illustration can also come in the form of denial. In my experience, as you continue to read this writing, that honesty has brought with me a certain amount of freedom, I could definitely attest that I have seen every form of deception and lie. Dishonesty brings a certain amount of guilt and it has always been the little ones that become exposed, and then a snowball of shit heap starts to build to cover up the previous one. My new wife had only admitted to me when we got to our humble home in West Virginia, that she had been the victim of molestation by her father. Here comes the desperate tap dance of desperation as I became enraged at the fact that she would have waited so long to tell me, nevertheless, waiting until we all relocated to West Virginia. This little white lie or discretionary exercise of waiting until the right time to disclose this, is an exercise in futility, if you ask me. Please forget all of the past traumas because I don't disclose them to many people, oh shit, I'm writing a memoir! Before I left Michigan to visit my soon-to-be widowed mother, I had a talk with my future in-laws about my intentions and plans with their daughter, and I did inform them of my past traumas with my daughter and myself, and to my dismay even then, all I got was a sympathetic pat on the shoulder as my future in-laws expressed their sorrow for my past. Not a word was uttered as we all celebrated holidays together with laughter and

Sherry. Card games and laughter could have been heard all throughout the Upper Peninsula of the great state of Michigan. Everyone was aware that I had just found out about all of this sexual abuse as I turned the tender age of forty. I can honestly say that I would not have even dated her if I knew that were the situation in her family. I am not qualified to make the psychological argument for what makes or breaks relationships, but I know that a woman that was physically, emotionally and sexually violated in the same way as I am should not be together. I am not much of a betting man, but I can make the argument that two people broken in the same exact way is not the foundation of a heathy relationship. As a child of abusive household, I think the percentage of a healthy home are in low single digits, and at this point I was just learning how to swim. Am I to be a lifeguard for a family of six, and get better for my three other biological children that need me?

The inevitability of our rapid separation took place within a week of January of 2019, Happy New Year everyone! I went to visit my dearest friend in Dallas, TX. I hadn't seen her in three years. She had always looked out for me in the past; she took off a weekend to help nurse me to health, she held me during my first flashback, had been my closest confidant during some of the most tumultuous times in my lifetime. I went there to try to find a friend and perhaps someone to confide the fact that I was getting divorced a second time. I had been experiencing a great deal of sexual inadequacy during my marriage, which had led me down some twisted roads of depravity. I did not have sex with my new wife. I knew it had to be very frustrating for her, in fact, she was so angry with me that one night she blurted out one night that she had sex with her ex-husband every day for the 16 years that they were married. Couple that with the two glasses of wine that she had, and the night was ruined. We would go through a myriad of sadness, grief, anger, rage, self-worth, and nothing was productive. Our time in the Midwest was one of the biggest steps back for us all. There are always two ways we can go in any given situation, and every action does indeed have a consequence. This unfortunate night left me with a nasty taste in my mouth. Here I was, a trauma victim, married to another child of molestation trying to make a second marriage work for both of us, with very similar sensitivities and tempers. I can't imagine what we put my beautiful children through. We struggled financially as both our parents tried to help keep us afloat financially, as I had hip and shoulder surgery, what a way to spend 10 out of 12 months in 2018. The rapid decline of western civilization was occurring right in front of our faces as these lifelong Michiganders would experience all of the hospitality of the best the Rust Belt had to offer. I would often go to any store or grocery store in our West Virginia community, and no one would offer any greeting there, unless to ask me where I was from. If my family and I would go out about town we took to keeping ourselves occupied with church and homeschooling. We were afraid to play in the rain as it was one of the most acidic places in America. One of the children informed me of that nugget of gold, that I could definitely do without. In rare instances that the folks of that wonderful county would speak to me, it was to ask where I was from or to hear my opinion of the current administration. It took my Latino surname a whopping 140 resume sends to get a job in

Pittsburg, PA; my wife only five resume sends in the same West Virginia town that we lived in. She got three job offers that I know of. The current administration had visited within one hundred miles of our small town at least five times in our short term of residency there that I recall. The only refuge I got was to be blessed to work in Pittsburgh, I loved the Steel City. I found great friends at the jobs I worked. Yes, two jobs I worked in the two months that I was marginally healthy in between surgeries on my hip and shoulder. The final two straws came in the last days of 2018, where my breaking point in this marriage for me came and I walked out at the most inappropriate time, yet again. The final two straws were the final argument that my wife, of this brief union and I had, and the comments made by my stepson, which to this day haunt me.

He said that his grandfather told him, "It's not a crime, if you don't get caught." I will let you draw your own conclusion about what that means to me and how I could leave another marriage behind, in such a brief time. That kind of comment, though, reminded me of my father who got away with it all his life, carried his pain everyday into his family that he was supposed to lead, and my father-in-law, that my soon-to-be ex-wife fought so hard to include in my life. That was her rationale for not telling me. The more manipulative statements were the last time we argued in December of 2018. She claimed I was crazy, that I just flipped a switch and that she couldn't understand me at all, even though she read the first draft I had written, and used everything I had written as a summation of who I was and would never be, as I left with five T-shirts, two pants, my guitar, and this laptop. How could any men leave another marriage, four beautiful children, without any furniture, in a beautiful four bedroom home, less than thirty minutes from South Padre Island, TX? This may or may not be unforgivable, although, I feel that I left on the best terms that I was capable of at the time, the last email I got from her stated that the Catholic church she attended, was taking the family, and had paid for her rent. I'm so glad that God took care of her as I sorted out my mind. I have come to the realization that I had to put myself first at all costs. My father-in-law sent me very scathing texts expressing that he had every right to judge me for leaving his daughter and grandchildren in such dire straits. I guess he had a right to be angry, but he definitely had no right to judge me. The truth is that we experience faith in two very distinct ways. I have no right to judge anyone, however, I know that we can see the fruits of our faith in the people that we encounter, the joy that we feel, and the love we give others. I tried, with grace, three times and begged him to ask his daughter about why I left. He said, he knew all he needed to know, and so begrudgingly I texted him as to how two men tore apart this marriage, as he sternly reminded me that no one man could overturn what God had brought together. I know and fully understand the vows I made. I made clear to another piece of shit that I couldn't stay in the marriage, due to the omissions that the entire family made, by omitting their truth, it is obvious that the fruits of our faith can only be judged by God. I am still waiting for a response. I guess it is never a crime if you don't get caught, but you (the royal you) will pay a price at some point, regardless the denomination you belong to, or the values you believe in. Whether you are an atheist, an agnostic, or faithful person,

I think love always wins out in the end. I took out a flyer on that forgive at that seventy times seventy thing that Jesus Christ died for, and you know what? I am banking on my ex-wife's forgiveness, and one day I will forgive her father and her. That is what I learned by attempting to forgive my own father. It is a process, and I am totally good with what I did. I'm fairly joyful most days, and truly free on the others, even when I randomly cry for no reason. I feel fairly strong when I shouldn't have a reason to live. Maybe Jesus was on to something, and if I can recommend anything to a survivor of any trauma – because Lord knows, I don't have the qualifications to give advice – it is that love and mercy can be the solution to all of the world's problems. To what plagues Israel and Palestine, the victims of trauma in my faith, the preacher and the victim, the addict and the family, the Caucasian and the colored, the gay and the straight, the pro-choice and the pro-life? I could go on and on with the problems that plague our world. As a good friend of mine says, who is yet another priest that has read the first manuscript in its infancy, told me to work on just sticking to affecting those that are in our own personal sphere. I heard you, and I did. I forgive the fuckers in my life, and I don't have to see them again. I don't have much regret, shame, or guilt. Isn't that the true enemy?

The faith could probably tell me that I can never marry again, but to tell you the truth, this dude will do his best to abide because I am faithful. It is my belief, as Father Becker told me, that I have died and entered the kingdom of heaven on earth. I fully believe that Father Becker knew me better than anyone else that I have ever allowed anyone inside my heart. I have had spiritual experiences that rock any orgasm

I have ever had. That has been the fruit of my belief system. I won't ever argue with anyone about which one is better, that is such a juvenile thing to do, but as you read the news these days, we aren't children of God, but Peter Pan's fighting with every captain we see, looking to fuck Tinker bell in the ass with a rusty metal dildo to compensate for our willingness to give forgiveness and love a chance.

I am left with the battle scars of a second failed marriage and the irony of that is that I think we had sex twice in this marriage. I am learning about myself sexually that what I need for a successful consummation. Now, that I will keep a secret! I must remain somewhat of a man of mystery if I ever fall in love again, and that is an exponential 'if' at this point. I will return to my experiences in 2019, thus far, I have been arrested twice on substance abuse issues, and had my car stolen. It was returned to me by the police two days later. Great job for our law enforcement, I am proud of the work they did even when I totaled my car.

There are times in a man's life, where if he does not get on with putting childish things behind him, he faces the prospect that he runs out of opportunities. I have had many chances at redemption, but the bottom line is that if I don't seize this moment, the cold fact is that I may not have another. I walked away from my totaled car in one piece, one April evening. The fact that I was able to survive with minimal injuries leaves me with nothing other than an appreciation for life and the total desire to see my children again. I'm really even not that angry anymore. I feel like this is the first time in my life that I have the proper knowledge of what I am facing, and how long the process of healing may take. I am also aware that it may get harder before it gets better, but I do have hope for the first time in my life. I have found that I am worth the work it takes to recover. In the past, I had always done it for family, children, marriages, work, and other external sources, where I had placed all my precious energy into. I am healing for myself. I love myself to make myself a priority. To slip into madness or a constant state of sorrow is not what has made this country great. In fact, quite conversely, we have endured. So what, if we don't have a great president? Does this mean it is the end of the world? Each time I start over, I feel like I lose a piece of me, but I'm still here.

It is important to keep in mind of the duality within us. To me, it is this free will that is given to us that encompasses us to love unconditionally and with mercy. I reiterate this theme over and over like an infomercial peddling a simple product. In a strange way, isn't the answer usually the simplest one? If we truly believe the major themes of the Bible, then vengeance is God's and God is love. I don't need to know much more than that. My mind can go from genius to village idiot in 2.4 seconds, so I have chosen to keep it simple. So, we have to keep our minds focused on simplicity in this world of glutinous information. We have to keep it simple in order to establish a truth and put aside foolish pride, because in the grand scheme of things mercy and love doesn't always look as perfect as our finite minds make it out to be. Certain elements around the world are threatening to undermine our God given free will, by flooding the information age with outright lies and half-truths, while aligning us like Crips and Bloods in the form of politics and war. Blame cannot be brought to the forefront to solve any problem, we know this, but if we are too rushed to judge and not listen we miss out on the point. My forgiveness of the worst is an ongoing struggle each day, while avoiding the cynicism that paralyzes us all. No one wants to be accountable to anyone. There is yet another split that is so painfully obvious to anyone around. There is this division for the whole world to see, and it is so emblematic of divisions that have kept man in an everlasting ignorance. There are idiot Catholics like Brett Kavanaugh, who I wouldn't entrust to babysit my children. And then there are brave people of faith that are repentant, love others without judgment, who include all in their hopes and dreams of community. Pride even dogs our fragmented political factions that believe that they are right. Have you ever been in a relationship with a person who was always right? How did that work out? I am not a theologian, just a man searching for answers, and I can't help but notice the pride that dogs predestination. That only a certain few can achieve salvation.

Since the Garden of Eden, we have been divided. What gives in a country founded by Puritanical principles? If we are a nation under God, and it has been defined in the Bible that God is love, then love is the solution. Love is clearly defined by Jesus as loving your neighbor as yourself. If we truly are out to fulfill the love and the prophets, we can surmise that one nation under God is one of love and tolerance of others. Making America great again is such a misnomer, because the promise of America cannot be quantified because our best is yet to come. I realize I made a bold statement, as we all face uncertainty and insecurity as to what we stand for as a nation. America has faced worse than our current administration. At least we aren't marching native peoples on foot from the East Coast to Oklahoma or walking around bragging about the number of our slaves. No matter how much the truth gets twisted or bent, one truth remains; our country will find its moral compass again, if we can ever figure out that we can't legislate morality. Man's law serves a different purpose than God's law, St Thomas Aquinas eloquently states; this is a fact I feel we can all agree on. What that means to me is this: God can only judge, and we can only accept one another like we accept ourselves, in our right to breathe, live and be happy. We cannot legislate a mother's womb by condemning her action on a baseline when we can't agree as to when life starts, or when two people are accountable for a pregnancy, why is there only legislation for the woman? When it clearly takes two to tango. I am a minority of a minority living as a Catholic in this country, and I am a part of a smaller minority who shares this opinion. Although, I have yet to meet a woman who doesn't feel terrible about having an abortion, I haven't seen a priest or nun that doesn't love them. We are confusing lifestyle with criminality, thus denying the fact that we can love or accept anyone from race, creed, drug use and sexuality. We cannot judge on a puritanical level because it limits the efforts of our forgiveness and ability to live as a community. I would think we have progressed as humans since the seventeenth century. Am I crazy for tossing these ideas out there? I just know that I don't have the power to judge anyone, if I am living by that golden rule. I have to forgive the worst, if I am to be forgiven. If I live a simple philosophy, then I can avoid the inevitable burnout and skip my next rehab or institution.

If there can be any void that is unattainable or in any human capacity to be completed, is that of a loss of a child's innocence. I understand that as uniquely as anyone can. What I mean by that, is that is that I am 44 and am still struggling with the fact that I have no idea what my identity is at this point. I can only imagine what it might be for someone of a lesser age. I cling to the hope of what I may be or the potential of what could've been. I write this in the hope that I may provide hope for my blood, my daughter, that she may find a way out of whatever she may encounter in her young life. That is the only thing that is keeping me alive. There is no solution other than the power of forgiveness and unconditional love. A heart that isn't closed off or open to the hope that things may improve for the better. The alternative is the eternal separation from a love eternal that leads to the pathway of redemption and a wisdom that unequivocally leads to a freedom that materials, sex or chemicals provide. There is no concrete ideology that leads to any sense of freedom that is given by a set of statures or law that enable the soul to be enlightened or free. There is unalienable right as the founding document of this great nation has stood for, for centuries and withstood civil unrest, recessions and depressions of an economic greed and minimalistic spiritual suicide that handicaps our progress. What every soul I have encountered has longed for, is the very thing that my faith has fought for and died for; meaning our saints and martyrs have died or reflected on in the face of unsurmountable odds. No matter how much they were defiled or vilified, they kept the faith, and that inspires me beyond any pain that I may endure now or in the future.